VISUAL™
Quick Tips

Wire Jewelry

VISUAL™
Quick Tips
Wire Jewelry

Visual®

by Chris Franchetti Michaels

WILEY

Wiley Publishing, Inc.

Library of Congress Control Number: 2008936353

ISBN: 978-0-470-34384-5

Printed in China

10   9   8   7   6   5

Book production by Wiley Publishing, Inc. Composition Services

Praise for the VISUAL Series

I just had to let you and your company know how great I think your books are. I just purchased my third Visual book (my first two are dog-eared now!) and, once again, your product has surpassed my expectations. The expertise, thought, and effort that go into each book are obvious, and I sincerely appreciate your efforts. Keep up the wonderful work!

—Tracey Moore (Memphis, TN)

I have several books from the Visual series and have always found them to be valuable resources.

—Stephen P. Miller (Ballston Spa, NY)

Thank you for the wonderful books you produce. It wasn't until I was an adult that I discovered how I learn—visually. Although a few publishers out there claim to present the material visually, nothing compares to Visual books. I love the simple layout. Everything is easy to follow. And I understand the material! You really know the way I think and learn. Thanks so much!

—Stacey Han (Avondale, AZ)

Like a lot of other people, I understand things best when I see them visually. Your books really make learning easy and life more fun.

—John T. Frey (Cadillac, MI)

I am an avid fan of your Visual books. If I need to learn anything, I just buy one of your books and learn the topic in no time. Wonders! I have even trained my friends to give me Visual books as gifts.

—Illona Bergstrom (Aventura, FL)

I write to extend my thanks and appreciation for your books. They are clear, easy to follow, and straight to the point. Keep up the good work! I bought several of your books and they are just right! No regrets! I will always buy your books because they are the best.

—Seward Kollie (Dakar, Senegal)

Credits

Acquisitions Editor
Pam Mourouzis

Development Editor
Donna Wright

Copy Editor
Marylouise Wiack

Technical Editor
Sandra Lupo

Editorial Manager
Christina Stambaugh

Publisher
Cindy Kitchel

Vice President and Executive Publisher
Kathy Nebenhaus

Interior Design
Kathie Rickard
Elizabeth Brooks

Cover Design
José Almaguer

Photography
Matt Bowen
Jodi Bratch (chapter opener image)

About the Author

Chris Franchetti Michaels is a writer and jewelry artisan specializing in beaded designs, wirework, and metal fabrication. She has written extensively about jewelry and jewelry making on the Internet since 2003, and she is the author of *Teach Yourself Visually: Jewelry Making & Beading* and *Beading Visual Quick Tips*. Chris has also appeared on several episodes of the DIY Network television show *Jewelry Making*, and her designs have been featured in popular jewelry project books. Visit her website BeadJewelry.net for more help and inspiration.

Acknowledgments

Thank you to Pam Mourouzis, Donna Wright, Marylouise Wiack, Matt Bowen, Sandra Lupo, and all the other team members whose many hours of work helped to make this book a practical and useful resource. As always, thanks also to Dennis for his continued support and encouragement.

Table of Contents

More Advanced Techniques   88

Wire Chains   148

Using a Wire Jig 162

Appendix:
References and Resources 194

Index 208

chapter 1

Jewelry Making Wire

Wire is available in many different types, sizes, colors, shapes, and metals. Use this chapter to review wire terminology and to learn how to determine which wire you should use for a given project.

Types of Jewelry Wire

You can make wire jewelry with just about any wire that is soft and easy to bend. Generally, the wire sold at bead shops or through jewelry supply companies for "wirework" or "wire wrapping" will work well, but so will some wire that you find at the hardware store. (See "Jewelry Wire Metals" on the next page.)

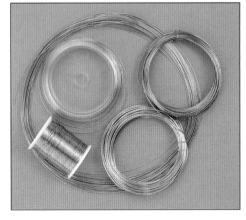

Wire that is labeled as "craft wire" may or may not be appropriate for jewelry making. Wire made mostly of copper, like much of the color-coated wire sold through craft stores, is easy to bend into the shapes of jewelry components (although its color coating can be scratched by your pliers or hammer). Wire that is made of tempered steel or other stiff metals, including some floral wire, is usually not recommended. (*Tempered* wire is wire that has been hardened; see "Wire Temper" on p. 12.)

When in doubt, try to obtain a sample of wire to experiment with. Also check the packaging or ask your supplier what material the wire is made from.

TIP

Do not confuse wire used for wire-jewelry making with *beading wire* (also called *bead stringing wire*). The wire used to make wire jewelry is solid metal, whereas beading wire is flexible, nylon-coated cable used for stringing beads but not for wrapping beads or constructing components.

Jewelry Wire Metals

Both *base metal* and *precious metal* wires are used in jewelry making. The most popular base metals are copper, plated copper, nickel, and brass. Precious metals include sterling silver, fine silver, and gold-filled metals (often called "gold-fill"). Some of these metals can *tarnish*, or take on a darker color over time. For information about polishing them, see "Polishing Techniques" on p. 204 in the Appendix.

COPPER WIRE

Copper is one of the best metals to work with because it's easy to bend into nicely rounded curves. It has a feel similar to sterling silver, but is much less expensive. This makes it a great metal to use for practice. You can also use copper wire to make prototypes, or experimental mock-ups, of new designs.

A potential downside of copper is that it tarnishes very easily. It may also develop a scaly green coating when it's exposed to excess moisture. In sufficient quantities, this coating, called *verdigris*, can be toxic. For this reason, some people prefer not to wear copper jewelry. At minimum, some people find that copper temporarily stains their skin if they wear it for long periods of time.

You can purchase copper wire from jewelry supply companies, wire manufacturers, bead stores, craft stores, and even hardware stores.

BRASS WIRE

Brass is an alloy, or mixture, of copper and zinc. It ranges in color from bright yellow to reddish-gold (often referred to as "red brass"). Brass wire tends to be less expensive than nickel silver (see p. 7), and similar in cost to copper.

Like pure copper, brass is prone to tarnishing. Many people like the look of darkened brass because it gives jewelry a more "antique" look.

CONTINUED ON NEXT PAGE

Brass wire is more difficult to work with than copper, nickel, silver, or gold. Although it is a soft metal, it tends to be stiffer than the others and resists bending as smoothly. However, it can be a nice alternative to more expensive metals, and you will find it easier to use with practice. Brass wire is sold through most jewelry supply companies and hardware stores, although the richer-colored "red brass" is usually only available through jewelry suppliers and wire manufacturers.

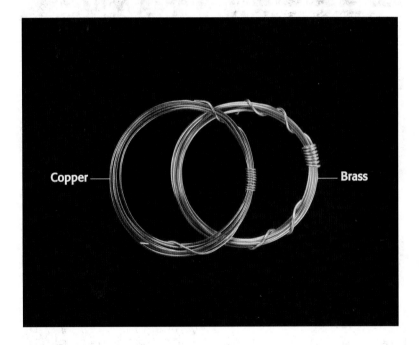

Copper ——————— ———— Brass

NICKEL-SILVER WIRE

Nickel silver is a base metal that is silver-colored but does not contain any precious silver; it is an alloy of copper, zinc, and nickel. It is much less expensive than silver, but can be slightly more expensive than copper.

Nickel silver has a somewhat dull-gray hue. Although it is a soft metal, it does not bend quite as smoothly as copper and sterling silver. Also keep in mind that many people are allergic to nickel, which can create redness or even a rash on their skin. For this reason, you may want to avoid it for jewelry that will be worn closely against the skin. Nickel silver is sold through most jewelry supply companies.

STERLING-SILVER WIRE

Sterling silver is an alloy of pure silver and copper. In wire form, it is soft and very easy to manipulate. Because sterling silver is a favorite jewelry metal, it's naturally one of the most common metals used in jewelry wirework. Unfortunately, it's also relatively expensive.

As you probably know, sterling silver is also prone to tarnishing. You can reduce tarnish by wearing sterling-silver jewelry often because the oils from your skin help to protect it from the air. To fight tarnish when your sterling-silver wire or jewelry is in storage, store it with anti-tarnish paper or wrap it in anti-tarnish fabric.

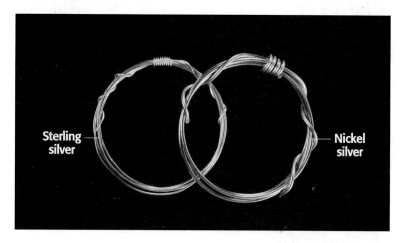

Sterling silver — Nickel silver

CONTINUED ON NEXT PAGE

GOLD AND GOLD-FILLED WIRE

You're probably familiar with gold. In addition to being a gorgeous metal for jewelry, it resists corrosion better than most metals, and it typically does not tarnish. Gold is normally alloyed with other metals to make it stronger. The amount of gold in a given piece of metal is denoted by its *karat*.

Karat gold is extremely expensive. A popular alternative is gold-filled wire, which is made up of an inner core of base metal covered with a relatively thick layer of real gold. Although gold-filled wire is usually more costly than sterling-silver wire, it's much less expensive than gold.

SILVER- AND GOLD-PLATED WIRE

Plated wire is usually solid copper wire that has been washed with a very thin coating of silver or gold. Although it is very affordable and has a nice look when it's brand new, it is not recommended for elaborate wirework. This is because the thin coating of silver or gold can scratch or rub off very easily. Try to use it sparingly or only as practice wire. If you do choose to use it, be aware that both silver- and gold-plated wire are prone to tarnish because of the high density of copper beneath the plating. To help protect again tarnish, look for plated wire labeled, "non-tarnish" or "tarnish-resistant."

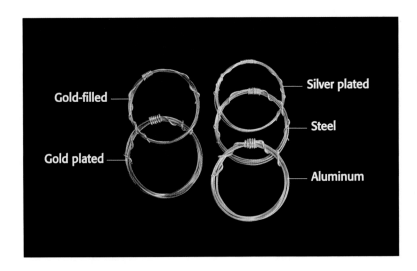

STEEL AND ALUMINUM WIRE

You can find wire made from steel and aluminum at most hardware stores. Steel wire is relatively hard but is still workable in smaller gauges, especially if it is annealed (see p. 12). Just be aware that larger gauges of steel can damage standard side cutters (see p. 22 in Chapter 2), and that steel is very prone to rusting. To avoid problems with rust, only use *stainless steel* wire for jewelry. Aluminum, on the other hand, is very soft—so soft that you can actually crush it with your pliers. Neither of these metals provides the color or shine of traditional jewelry wire, but you can experiment with them to make unusual and more cost-effective designs.

TIP

You can order pre-made jump rings made from steel and aluminum through chain-mail jewelry supply Web sites. To find them, try searching for the terms "chain mail jump rings" or "maille jump rings" on the Internet.

Wire is manufactured by pulling (or "drawing") metal through a hole in a hard metal plate. The shape of that hole determines the shape of the wire. The most common wire shape is *round*. Round wire is especially versatile because its appearance is not affected by minor twisting. To give round wire a twisted appearance intentionally, you can twist two strands of round wire together (see p. 99).

Square wire is also popular for jewelry making. Because it has flat sides, you can stack square wires on top of one another to create the look of a striated, solid piece of metal. Square wire can also be made to look more ornate by twisting it as a single strand (see p. 97).

Half-round wire is rounded (or "domed") on one side, and flat on the other. It is often wrapped around stacks of square wire, flat-side down, to hold the square wires securely together.

Triangle wire has three equal, flat sides. You can use it in place of half-round wire for wrapping, or to create unusual-looking components. Like square wire, triangle wire can also be twisted as a single strand.

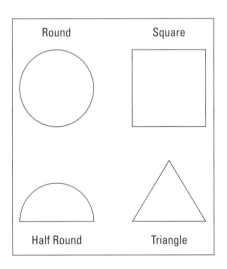

Round   Square

Half Round   Triangle

Wire Gauge

Wire size is denoted by a number called *gauge*: the larger the number, the thinner the wire; and the smaller the number, the thicker the wire. The chart on p. 196–197 in the Appendix provides the approximate diameters of the most popular American Wire Gauges (also called AWG) for jewelry making, and suggested uses for each. You can use this chart as a starting point for determining which gauge of wire to use for a particular project. The most common gauges used for wire jewelry are in the 26- to 16-gauge range.

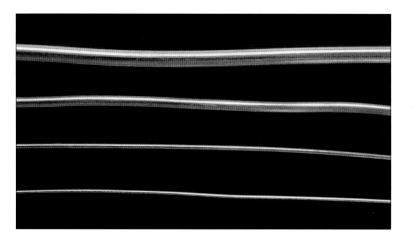

TIP

Keeping Track of Wire Gauge
You may notice that there are very small size differences between one gauge and the next. When you purchase wire, the gauge should be indicated on the spool or package. However, you will often find stray pieces of wire, of various gauges, strewn across your work area. Consider purchasing a *wire gauge plate* so that you can measure and organize scrap wire for proper reuse (see "Measuring Tools" on p. 33.) Once you've determined the gauge of a piece of wire, you should mark it for future reference. Fold a small piece of masking tape around one end, and mark it with the gauge using a permanent marker.

Temper refers to the hardness, or stiffness, of wire. Wire with *soft temper* is easier to bend than wire with *hard temper.* Base-metal wire is rarely labeled with its temper; but when you buy sterling-silver wire, you have a selection of tempers to choose from. Sterling-silver wire with *dead-soft* temper is the most versatile for jewelry making because it's the easiest to work with. However, you may want to use *half-hard* sterling wire when you'd like your finished component to be relatively stiff. For example, jump rings or ear wires are more durable when they're made from wire with half-hard temper.

You can manually increase the temper of wire by hammering it. When you tap on wire with a hammer, the molecules align so that the metal becomes stiffer. (To learn more about hammering tools and supplies, see Chapter 2.)

Temper can be softened by a process called *annealing*. This is often done by heating the wire to a specific temperature using a torch or kiln, and then cooling it in a controlled manner. If you plan to use steel wire in your designs, it's best to select annealed steel to ensure that it will be soft enough to work with.

TIP

Temper and Wire Breakage

Temper is also increased when wire is repeatedly bent. In fact, the more you bend a piece of wire back and forth, the stiffer and more brittle it becomes, which can cause the wire to break. For this reason, always avoid over-manipulating wire. If a component begins to feel very stiff or fragile as you work with it, you should discard it and create a new one.

You can, however, gently bend wire back and forth to purposely make it stiffer. This technique is often used to increase the security of dead-soft jump rings. If you gently open and close a dead-soft jump ring two or three times, it will be less likely to come open by itself; if you open it too wide or open and close it many times repeatedly, it will break.

Wire Finishes and Treatments

Some wire materials are prone to tarnishing, or darkening, over time as they are exposed to the air. You can clean and polish your wire and wirework designs for a bright, shiny finish (see the next section, "Wire Care"), allow them to darken naturally, or intentionally darken them using chemicals to create an oxidized or "antiqued" look. (Refer to "Oxidization Methods" in the Appendix for more information about these techniques.)

Wire that has been treated or manufactured to resist oxidation is also available. Examples include "tarnish-resistant" copper and plated wire (which is typically coated), and the Argentium brand of sterling-silver wire (which has been chemically altered to inhibit oxidation). Consider using these wires when you want to create jewelry that will remain bright and shiny over time.

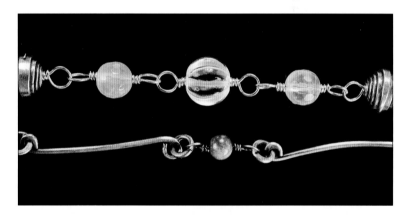

TIP

Keep in mind that any surface-treatment coating, whether to protect wire from tarnishing or to add color, can be damaged by your wirework tools. Always manipulate this wire gently with your pliers, and use nylon-jaw, taped, or coated pliers if possible.

Here are some tips for keeping your wire, and wire jewelry, clean and in good condition.

CLEANING

It's a good idea to clean your wire jewelry after you complete a design. This removes any oils or debris that accumulated on the wire during construction. Jewelry cleaning products that contain small amounts of ammonia work well for most jewelry. You can usually find them at drug stores, sold as plastic containers of transparent, blue liquid. Dip the jewelry into the liquid and then use a very soft brush (like an infant toothbrush) to gently scrub all of the wire components in the design. Rinse and thoroughly dry your jewelry before wearing or storing it.

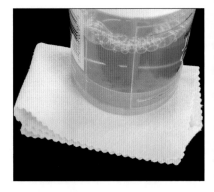

POLISHING

Although cleaning will brighten your jewelry and add sparkle, it will not remove unwanted tarnish. To remove tarnish from your wire or wire jewelry, you need to *polish* it. Common polishing methods include using a *jewelry polishing cloth*, *silver-polishing paste* or *cream*, or (for finished jewelry) a *rotary tumbler* that is designed for tumbling rocks. Copper wire can also be polished using household vinegar or lemon juice. (See "Polishing Techniques" in the Appendix.)

TIP

Before using any cleaning or polishing chemical on your jewelry, check the product packaging to make sure it is intended for use on all of the materials your jewelry contains. For example, if a design includes softer gemstone beads or pearls, they could be damaged by ammonia-based cleaners and polishing compounds.

STORAGE

Wire tends to oxidize more quickly when it's exposed to the air. To protect your wire and jewelry from tarnish, it is best to store it inside sealed plastic bags or jewelry pouches made from tarnish-resistant cloth. You can also purchase tarnish-resistant paper tabs or strips that you can store with your jewelry inside a bag or pouch. These little papers contain chemicals that help keep metal from oxidizing. Alternatively, consider using a jewelry box lined with tarnish-resistant fabric, or make your own pouches or lined storage containers using tarnish-resistant fabric from a fabric store.

Keep in mind that wire and wire jewelry usually resist tarnish, to some degree, after they have been polished with a polishing cloth, paste, or liquid, because some of the polishing compound remains on the surface of the metal. This is especially true if you buff your jewelry with a clean cloth after polishing, rather than fully cleaning it.

GENERAL TIPS

Finally, be sure to always handle your handmade wire jewelry gently, and protect it from harsh chemicals (especially household bleach), moisture, or situations where it could easily become damaged. Wire components can be pulled apart, stretched, bent out of shape, and even weakened if they are snagged or crushed. If you care for your wire jewelry as you would fine jewelry, it should give you years of use and enjoyment.

chapter 2

Wirework Tools

With a basic set of tools, you can transform wire into beautiful jewelry. The most important wirework tools are chain nose pliers, round nose pliers, flat nose pliers, and wire cutters. This chapter describes these tools, along with some others that will be useful additions to your tool kit.

You can find wirework pliers at most bead stores and through jewelry supply companies. Similar pliers are often sold at hardware stores, but those pliers tend to be too large for accurate wirework or have inappropriate features (like serrated jaws instead of smooth ones). Keep in mind that more expensive pliers generally are of better quality and will last much longer than inexpensive pliers.

CHAIN NOSE PLIERS

Chain nose pliers have flat jaws that are thinner at the tips and wider at the base. You can use them to make precise bends in wire, hold wire components while you work, and press down wire coils. Some models have straight jaws, while others (often called bent nose pliers) are curved. It's important to use chain nose pliers that have smooth jaws—not serrated jaws—for wirework. Serrated (or textured) jaws can create undesirable impressions on soft metals.

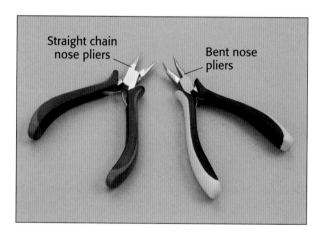

Straight chain nose pliers

Bent nose pliers

TIP

Chain nose pliers are available in a range of jaw sizes. For intricate wirework using smaller-gauge wire, select pliers that are very narrow at the tips.

FLAT NOSE PLIERS

Flat nose pliers, which are used for bending and holding wire, have long, flat, rectangular jaws. As with chain nose pliers, it's important to use a pair with smooth jaws. Flat nose pliers are available in different widths and lengths, but any standard beginner's pair works well for most applications.

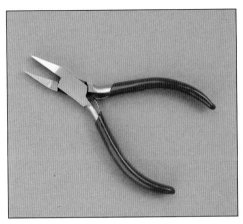

ROUND NOSE PLIERS

Round nose pliers, which are used to create loops in wire, have jaws that are rounded into solid, graduated cylinders. You can find round nose pliers with very long noses at the hardware store, but shorter-nose versions are better for jewelry making.

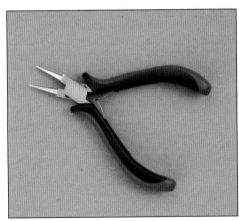

TIP

Like chain nose pliers, round nose pliers are available in a range of sizes, or jaw widths. Use larger sizes to make larger wire loops and with larger-gauge wire, but opt for smaller sizes to make very small loops or when using small gauges of wire.

CONTINUED ON NEXT PAGE

NYLON JAW PLIERS

Nylon jaw pliers are special pliers with plastic jaws. You can use them to hold wire without risk of scratching it, and to straighten bent wire. After a while, the nylon jaws will wear out, but most models have removable nylon inserts that you can replace.

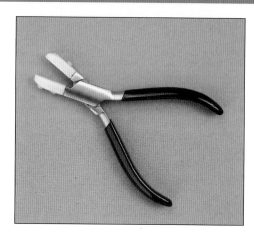

To straighten wire using nylon jaw pliers, hold one end of the wire (or the spool, as shown) securely with your fingers or with chain nose pliers, grasp the wire with the nylon jaw pliers, and then pull the nylon jaw pliers along the entire length of the wire. Repeat this process until the wire is straight enough to work with. Keep in mind, however, that straightening wire usually increases its temper, making it a little more difficult to work with and slightly more brittle (see the section, "Wire Temper," in Chapter 1).

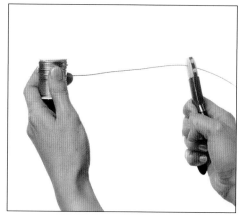

OTHER WIREWORK PLIERS

Although most tasks can be completed using chain nose, round nose, flat nose, and/or nylon jaw pliers, you may find it helpful to use more specialized pliers in some situations. For example, *half-round pliers* (also called *forming pliers*), which have one rounded jaw and one flat jaw, can be used to make large bends in wire like those required for ear wires. Another specialty model, called *stepped round nose pliers*, provides three different precise jaw sizes in one pair, making it easier to create wire loops of exactly the same size. You can experiment with these and other specialty models to see whether they help you work faster or more efficiently.

TIP

Determining the Quality of Pliers

High-quality jewelry pliers last longer and typically are more comfortable to use than lower-quality pliers. Here are some characteristics to look for when shopping for a high-quality pair:

- Pliers with jaws made of *hardened steel* are stronger and may be less likely to mar wire than pliers made from *stainless steel*.

- *Box joints* provide pliers with better alignment between their jaws and tend to be more stable than *lap joints*.

- Some pliers have wide, ergonomically designed handles that reduce hand and wrist fatigue and make it easier to work with precision.

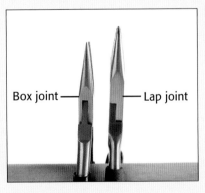

Box joint ——————— Lap joint

Wire cutters essentially are pliers with sharp blades for jaws. As with pliers, the wire cutters sold at bead stores and by jewelry supply companies are more suitable for jewelry making than those you typically find at hardware stores.

SIDE CUTTERS

Side cutters (also called *side flush cutters*) are wire cutters that are designed to make *flush cuts* on wire. A flush cut is a relatively straight, flat cut that looks nicer and is less prone to snagging or scratching than a jagged, or "beveled," cut.

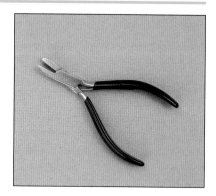

TIP

The Importance of Maximum Cutting Capacity

Most cutters are labeled with their *maximum cutting capacity*, which is an indicator of the types and sizes of wire the cutters can cut without being damaged. Maximum cutting capacity is usually expressed as the maximum gauge of a specific wire material that the cutters will safely cut. For example, if your cutters are labeled "18-gauge copper," you should only use them on 18-gauge or smaller wire that is no harder than copper wire. Because sterling silver and brass are similar in hardness to copper, you should be able to safely use them on those metals. However, hardened steel wire would likely mar the blades of these pliers.

OTHER WIRE CUTTERS

Although side cutters are adequate for most wire jewelry making projects, many jewelry supply companies offer a range of specialty cutters that can be useful in certain situations. For example, *end cutters* have blades that run perpendicular, rather than parallel, to the handles of the pliers. They allow you to hold the pliers at a more comfortable angle when trimming very short lengths of wire. *Double flush cutters* are pliers that create a flush cut on both ends of the wire created by the cut. They eliminate the need to turn your pliers around to make a second cut when you need a flush cut on both ends, such as when you make jump rings using pliers (see p. 42 in Chapter 4).

TIP

How to Make a Flush Cut

To make a flush cut using side cutters as shown in the photo on the right, trim the wire with the flat side of the jaws facing the wire component and the beveled side of the jaws facing the end of the wire that you are cutting off.

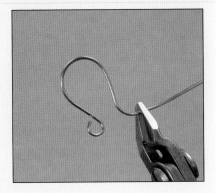

You can use a hammer to flatten and harden wire and some wire jewelry components.

CHASING HAMMER

The *chasing hammer* is a popular hammer for wirework. It's actually designed for hammering on other tools (called *chasing tools*) to create marks on sheet metal, but it also works well for flattening and hardening wire. For best results, it is important to select a chasing hammer with a *face,* or hammering surface, that is both smooth and slightly domed. Chasing hammers with perfectly flat faces have edges that can mar your wire. As an alternative, you can use either a *jeweler's ball-peen hammer,* which has a beveled face, or a *riveting hammer* (traditionally used for securing rivets in sheet metal), which usually has a slightly rounded face. These hammers are sold by most jewelry making supply companies.

NYLON HEAD HAMMER

A *nylon head hammer* has a head and/or face made of plastic. Because plastic is softer than metal, it will not scratch or mar your wire; however, it also will not flatten it as much as a chasing hammer will. Use a nylon head hammer when you want to increase the temper of your wire (stiffen it), or to straighten a wire component that has become bent.

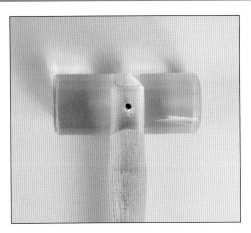

RAWHIDE HAMMER

A *rawhide hammer* (also called a *rawhide mallet*) has a head made of natural rawhide. Just like a nylon head hammer, a rawhide hammer will not scratch or mar your wire. Also, because rawhide is softer and has more "give" than plastic, it absorbs more of the impact of hammering. This creates less bounce and makes it more comfortable to use. Use a rawhide hammer to slightly harden the temper of wire or to flatten bent components.

TIP

The rawhide used to make rawhide hammers is similar to that used to make some dog chew toys. To protect your hammer from chewing damage, never leave it in a place where it is accessible to dogs.

Bench Blocks and Bench Pins

Although bench blocks and bench pins have similar names, they are actually quite different tools. One provides a surface for hammering, and the other is a brace that jewelers use to stabilize their work. Both are available through jewelry supply companies.

BENCH BLOCK

A *bench block* is a smooth piece of hardened steel used as a surface for hammering. You place wire on top of the bench block and hold it in place while you hammer. To keep your bench block from moving while you hammer, try placing it on a rubberized beading mat.

BENCH PIN

A *bench pin* is a specially shaped piece of solid wood that jewelers attach to their work benches. They use it to support pieces of metal while cutting and filing. You can also

Bench block   Bench pin

use one to stabilize your wire coil when making jump rings with a jeweler's saw (see p. 46 in Chapter 4). Many bench pins fit within pre-made slots found in jewelers' benches, but others can be attached to any work surface using a clamp.

Mandrels are used to wrap wire into particular shapes. The most common mandrels are metal rods for coiling wire or forming wire loops. You can purchase mandrels in various sizes and shapes through jewelry supply companies, or you can make your own. Household objects like pens, chopsticks, and prescription bottles can serve as mandrels. You can even make mandrels out of wooden dowels or small metal tubes from a hardware store. A *tapered mandrel* is a special type of mandrel that allows you to create wire shapes in a range of sizes. Shapes created near the end of the mandrel are smaller than those created near the base. A common type of tapered mandrel is the *ring mandrel,* which is used for making finger rings in specific sizes. Some ring mandrels have a channel on one side where a bead can rest when you make a wire-and-bead ring (see "Wrapped Bead Ring" on p. 128 in Chapter 5).

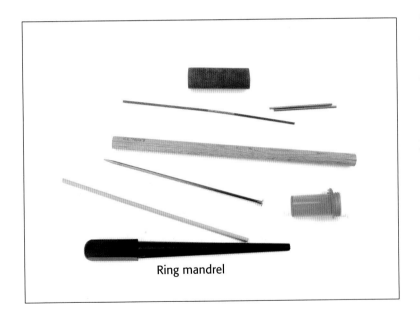

Ring mandrel

A *wire jig* is a device for guiding wire into specific shapes. It consists of a flat surface, or *base,* and a number of *pegs* that fit into the base. (Most modern pre-made jigs have moveable pegs that you can arrange in several configurations.) You can create jewelry components in useful shapes by wrapping wire around the pegs. When you make multiples of the same component, each will be the same shape and size. Jigs are available in many sizes and styles. Some are made of plastic, but the more durable models are made of metal. You can find them at some bead shops and through most jewelry supply companies.

Wire-Twisting Tools

Twisted wire has a more ornate look than straight wire. Here are the most common tools used to make those twists. To review the techniques for twisting wire, see "Twist Wire" in Chapter 5.

HAND DRILL

A *hand drill* is a manual drill that operates when you turn a crank handle on its side. You can use it to twist together two strands of round wire. Simple hand drills are sometimes stocked by hardware stores, but you can find one specifically for crafting (like the one in the example) at many craft stores.

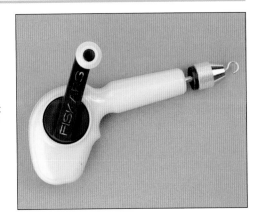

PIN VICE

A *pin vice* is a small metal pipe with a clamp at one end. You can use it to grasp and twist square wire. Pin vices are available through jewelry supply companies and at hobby shops.

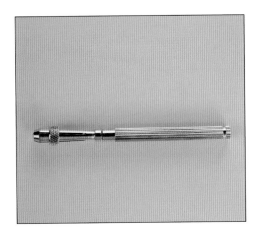

A *jeweler's saw* is a special saw designed for intricately cutting sheet metal, but you can also use it to speed the process of making multiple jump rings (see "Make and Use Jump Rings" in Chapter 4). Most hardware stores carry simple, affordable jeweler's saws, and higher-quality models are available through jewelry supply companies.

THE BASIC SAW

A jeweler's saw is a type of *coping saw*. It is made up of a metal frame that holds a thin metal blade. The blade is held in place by removable bolts or clamps at either end of the frame. Jeweler's saw blades are available in a variety of sizes. You can use a size 2 blade for 16- or 18-gauge jump rings, and a size 1 blade for 20-gauge jump rings.

To properly use a jeweler's saw, run the blade back and forth over the metal or wire slowly and smoothly with very light pressure, keeping the saw straight—not tilted to one side or the other. For best results, run your jeweler's saw blade across a block of *beeswax* or *blade lubricant* before sawing.

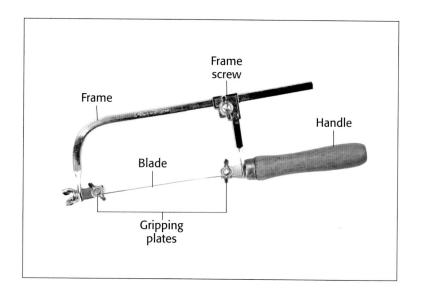

Frame screw

Frame

Handle

Blade

Gripping plates

There is more than one method for setting up a jeweler's saw, and some saw models require different techniques than others. (Check with your saw's manufacturer for their recommendations.) Generally, you need to secure both ends of the saw blade into clamps called *gripping plates* at both ends of the saw frame, with the teeth of the blade facing up and pointing toward the handle, and then adjust the tension of the frame so that the blade is held taut. Here are two possible approaches.

PULLING THE BLADE TAUT

1 Insert the blade into the gripping plate that is closest to the handle, and then tighten the gripping plate screw or clamp.

2 Insert the other end of the blade into the other gripping plate, and then tighten that screw or clamp.

3 Loosen the *frame screw* at the back of the frame, and use both hands to pull the ends of the frame away from each other as far as they will go.

4 Rest the back of the frame against your leg or work surface (with the handle pointing down) to preserve the tension, and re-tighten the frame screw.

"SPRINGING" THE BLADE TAUT

Before using this method, make sure that your saw frame is adjusted so that the space between the gripping plates is slightly shorter than the length of the saw blade. (If necessary, loosen the frame screw, adjust the frame, and then re-tighten the frame screw.)

1 Insert one end of the blade into the gripping plate nearest the handle, and tighten its screw or clamp.

2 Position the saw between your chest and a solid work table or bench, with the blade facing upward and the handle touching your chest.

3 Lean forward and push the ends of the frame toward one another.

4 Insert the second end of the blade into the other gripping plate, and tighten its screw or clamp.

5 Lean back and release the pressure on the blade to allow the blade to "spring" taut.

TIP

Whichever method you use, make sure that the saw blade "rings," almost like a guitar string, when you strum it with your fingernail. If it doesn't, readjust the frame to increase its tension on the blade.

Needle Files

Needle files are small metal files that come in a variety of shapes. The most useful shape for wirework is the *flat needle file.* You can use this file to smooth the ends of wire after cutting it. Affordable needle files are stocked by many hardware stores. If you'd like one that lasts longer or is more comfortable to use, you can purchase one through a jewelry supply company.

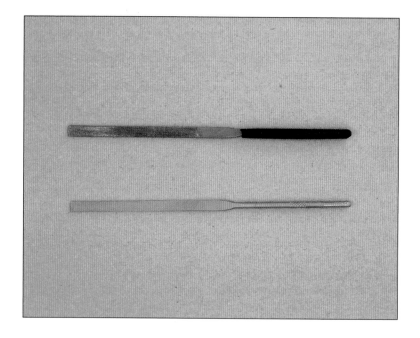

TIP

Your needle files will last longer if you always file in the same direction. Always run the file over your wire in a direction moving away from you, rather than toward you, and never file in a back-and-forth motion.

For many jewelry projects, you need to measure lengths of wire and determine the dimensions of jewelry components. You may also need to confirm the gauges of wire you have on hand. Here are some basic tools to help you make fast and accurate measurements as you work.

GENERAL MEASURING TOOLS

It's a good idea to have a ruler and a measuring tape on hand for measuring the lengths of beaded strands, sizing beads and other components, and sizing jewelry. You can also use a sliding *brass measuring gauge* to determine the dimensions of beads and components. Brass measuring gauges have marks that line up to show you measurements in millimeters and inches. They are relatively inexpensive and provide very accurate measurements.

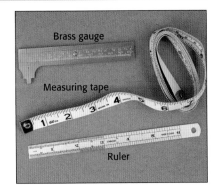

Brass gauge

Measuring tape

Ruler

WIRE GAUGE PLATES

It may be difficult to tell the exact gauge of a piece of wire just by looking at it, and so it's a good idea to invest in a disc-shaped measuring device called a *wire gauge plate*.

To use it, insert a piece of wire into a slot along the edge of the gauge. (Do not pass it through the round hole.) Move the wire from slot to slot until you find the one that most snugly fits it. The number stamped near that slot is the gauge, or approximate gauge, of your wire.

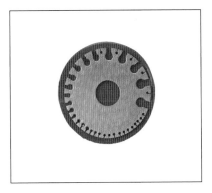

chapter 3

Safety, Storage, and Organization

In addition to wire and wirework tools, you should also invest in some basic supplies for wirework safety and for proper storage and organization.

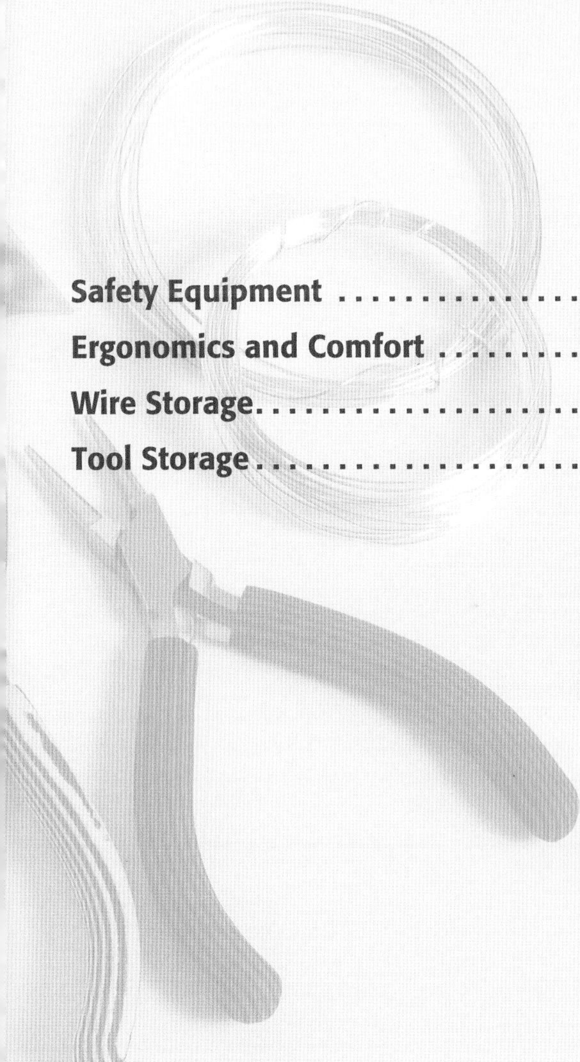

Wire-jewelry making is not a high-risk activity, but it's a good idea to take some basic measures for safety and comfort. Here are the most important safety devices to have on hand in your work area.

EYE PROTECTION

When you trim wire with wire cutters, little pieces of wire will fly out across your work area or even across the room. Because you don't want any of these pieces of wire flying into your eyes, be sure to wear safety glasses as often as possible when you work. Also, always be extra careful when other people or pets are in the room.

You should also wear safety glasses when you hammer wire. Although it's rare for pieces of wire to fly up during hammering, a piece of your hammer or bench block could shatter and become airborne. Again, although this shouldn't happen very often, if at all, don't take the risk.

EAR PROTECTION

Basic wirework doesn't require the use of noisy mechanical tools or equipment. However, you may find that hammering on a bench block can be uncomfortable for your eardrums. Keep some earplugs or earmuff-style ear protectors near your hammer and bench block, and wear them whenever you need to make more than one or two taps on larger-gauge wire.

TIP

One way to keep wire from flying dangerously through the air is to hold your wire and side cutters close to your work surface when you make a cut, and angle the beveled side of the pliers' jaws slightly downward.

Wire-jewelry making involves intricate, sometimes repetitive work using relatively small hand tools. Here are some steps you can take to reduce hand fatigue and eye strain.

1. Sit in a comfortable chair that has adequate lumbar back support. Always maintain a straight, supported posture, and avoid slouching or hunching over.

2. Use chair armrests that are high enough to support your arms, or sit at a work table that is the proper height for resting your arms and elbows. (An adjustable-height chair makes this easier.)

3. Keep all of your basic tools and supplies within easy reach of your work area. Avoid twisting and turning in your chair as much as possible.

4. Do not perform the same type of technique for an extended period of time. If your hands or wrists begin to feel stiff or cramped, stop and take a break.

5. Ensure that you have adequate lighting over your work area. You will need very bright light that is not irritating because of blinking or excessive heat production. You may want to invest in one or more lamps that are designed specifically for craft work.

6. Use a hands-free magnifier when you do intricate work using small-gauge wire and components. A *headband magnifier* is the kind worn by jewelers; it fits over your head and has magnifying lenses that flip up when you're not using them. You can also use a table-top magnifier or a magnifier that attaches to your lamp.

7. Consider using pliers with special "ergonomic" handles. They are much more comfortable to use than pliers with narrow, thinly coated handles.

8. Keep a small first-aid kit in your work area. It will come in handy if you accidentally prick or scratch a finger.

Be sure to store unused wire in a place where it is protected from both moisture and excess exposure to air. This is especially important for wire that is prone to tarnishing, like copper, brass, and sterling silver, and wire that is susceptible to rust and corrosion, like steel. Consider keeping coils of wire in sealable plastic bags labeled with the wire's material, temper, and gauge. (For best protection, purchase sturdy, plastic storage bags through a jewelry supply company rather than using food storage bags from the grocery store.)

To organize your wire, keep the plastic bags in labeled plastic boxes, or "file" them in large envelopes in hanging file folders. By labeling the folders, you will have easy access to the exact type, shape, and gauge of wire you need, when you need it.

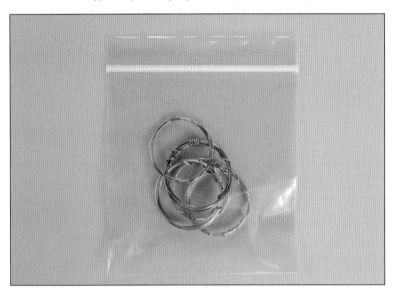

There are a lot of options for storing your wirework tools so that they are protected from damage but also easily accessible. Jewelry supply companies carry tabletop stands that hold multiple pairs of pliers and cutters upright by their handles. Hardware stores sell long magnetic strips that attach to the wall and are strong enough to hold steel pliers, needle files, and even bench blocks. Alternatively, you can store your tools flat in labeled plastic boxes, or upright in re-used coffee cans. If you need portable tool storage, look for an affordable plastic tool box at a hardware store or a roomy tackle box (with a large compartment for tools) at a sporting goods store.

However you store your tools, do your best to protect them from moisture. This is especially important for pliers and cutters made from hardened steel, which is prone to rust. To further protect steel tools, try coating them occasionally with paste wax.

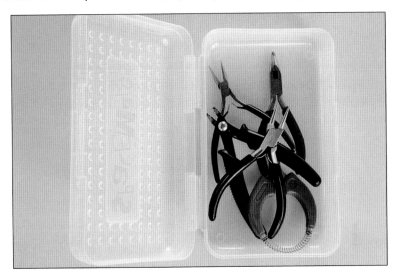

chapter 4

Basic Wirework

You can use basic wirework techniques to create essential jewelry components like jump rings, head and eye pins, bead drops and links, clasps, and ear wires.

Make and Use Jump Rings

Save money by making your own jump rings in the sizes and quantities you need. You can make them from pieces of scrap wire or use wire directly from the spool or coil. For wire gauge recommendations, see the chart on p. 196–197.

USE PLIERS TO MAKE JUMP RINGS

Use this technique when you only need to make a few jump rings at a time. Begin by making a wire coil, and then cut each coil to create a ring.

1 Grasp the end of the wire with round nose pliers at the point along the jaws that matches what you'd like the inside diameter of your jump rings to be.

2 Holding the base of the wire with your fingers, rotate your wrist away from you to roll the wire into a loop.

3 Remove the pliers and re-insert them into the new loop in their original position.

4 Begin rolling the wire away from you again while using the thumb and index finger of your other hand to position the new loop *below* the first loop on the pliers.

5 Position this new loop up against the first loop to make a short wire coil.

6 Continue using your thumb to guide the wire while using the pliers to make repeated coils at the same place on the nose of the pliers. The coils will move toward the tips of the pliers as you create them.

7 Stop when you have created at least one more coil than the number of jump rings you need.

8 Use side cutters to trim off the tip of the first coil.

Note: *To create a flush cut with regular side cutters, be sure that the flat side of the cutters is facing away from the end of the wire.*

CONTINUED ON NEXT PAGE

9   Turn the cutters around so that their flat side is facing the opposite direction, and use the cutter tips to cut through the coil just above your first cut. Your first jump ring should fall off the coil.

10 Trim off the next tip of wire with the flat side of the cutters facing away from the tip (to make a flush cut).

11 Continue cutting all of your rings from the coil, turning your pliers each time to ensure a flush cut.

TIP

Creating Consistently Sized Rings and Loops

The jaws of round nose pliers are graduated in diameter; they're smallest at the tips and thickest at the base. This allows you to choose how large of a ring or loop you'd like to make. You can grasp the wire closer to the tips for a smaller loop or closer to the base for a larger one.

To help you make consistently sized loops for a given project, try marking the point you're using on the pliers with a permanent marker. (These markers are not really "permanent" on metal; the mark will wear off.)

As an alternative, affix a small piece of masking tape to the nose of the pliers, with one edge of the tape marking the spot.

USE A MANDREL TO MAKE RINGS

You can make more jump rings in less time by using a mandrel to create the coil. This basic coiling technique is also used for making double-wrapped wire beads in Chapter 5.

1 Hold the wire perpendicular to the mandrel with about an inch of wire remaining on one side.

2 Use your thumb to hold the wire securely against the mandrel, and hold the other end of the wire with your other hand.

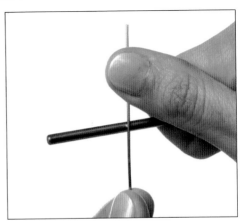

3 Rotate your wrist to turn the mandrel slowly and begin making the first coil, positioning your thumb gently against the 1-inch tail of wire for leverage.

4 Continue turning the mandrel to make coils, using your other hand to position each new coil up against the previous coil.

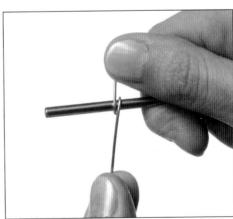

CONTINUED ON NEXT PAGE

5 Complete at least one more coil than the number of jump rings you'd like to make, up to a maximum of about 1 inch of coil.

6 Slowly pull the coil off of the mandrel, being careful not to open any spaces between coils.

7 Perform Steps 8–11 of "Use Pliers to Make Jump Rings" (p. 42) to create each jump ring.

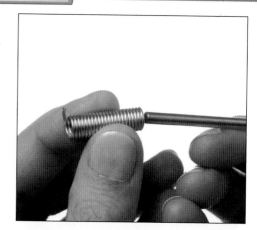

CUT JUMP RINGS WITH A SAW

Rather than cutting each jump ring individually, you can cut through several at a time using a jeweler's saw. This technique takes some practice, so try it first with scrap wire and experiment with holding both the coil and the saw at slightly different angles. For information on a bench pin and setting up a jeweler's saw, see p. 26 and 30–31 in Chapter 2.

1 Using a wire coil that is about 1 inch long, hold the coil between your fingers and against a secured bench pin (or other block of wood).

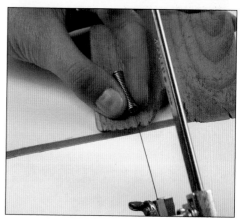

② Run the saw backwards along the top of the first coil a few times to create a small groove.

③ Keeping the blade in that groove, slowly and gently saw into the first and second coils.

④ Continue sawing slowly, in a straight line, until you have cut through the entire coil. Do not press down; allow the weight of the saw to do the work.

Note: The last few coils may start to fall over when you reach them. If that happens, hold them securely with your fingers to complete your cut. The jump rings will fall off as you cut them.

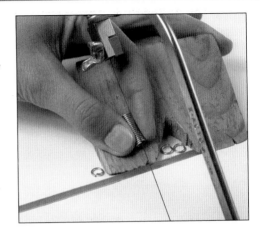

TIP

As you cut jump rings with a saw, the cut rings will fall down beneath the bench pin. To keep from losing them, place a tray or empty plastic storage box beneath the edge of your work surface to catch them.

CONTINUED ON NEXT PAGE

OPEN AND CLOSE JUMP RINGS

It is important to open and close jump rings correctly, to keep them from breaking or coming loose during wear.

To open a jump ring, hold it in front of you using two pairs of chain nose or flat nose pliers, with the ring-opening facing upward. Gently twist one end of the ring toward you and the other end away from you.

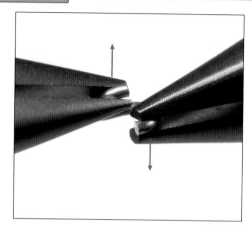

To close a jump ring, twist the ends back in the opposite direction, and wiggle them together until the ring is completely closed.

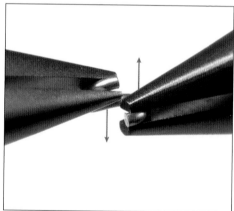

TIP

Never pull or push the ends of a jump ring with a side-to-side motion. This can weaken the metal, deform the ring's shape, and prevent it from closing properly.

Hammer Jump Rings

You can increase the temper of wire (that is, make it stiffer) and give wire components a more finished look by gently hammering them. Here is the basic technique for hammering jump rings.

1. Place a jump ring on a clean bench block, with the ring-opening facing you.

2. Use a chasing hammer to tap the jump ring, with the hammer angled slightly down toward the side of the jump ring that is opposite its opening (the side facing away from you).

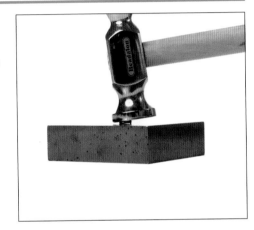

By hammering at this angle, you create a ring that is slightly more flattened on one side than the other. This stiffens the jump ring without flattening down the opening, leaving it easy to open and close.

Manufacturers use special machinery to create head pins with tiny nail heads on the ends, but you can create simpler wire head pins that work just as well. For wire gauge recommendations, see the chart on p. 196–197.

SIMPLE HEAD PINS

① Use side cutters to cut a length of wire for each head pin that you'd like to make. Each should be about ³⁄₁₆ inch to ¼ inch longer than you'd like the straight part of the finished pin to be.

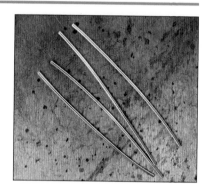

② Trim the tips of each wire with side cutters (as needed) to ensure straight, flush-cut ends.

③ Use the very tips of round nose pliers to create a tiny loop at one end of each wire.

④ Use chain nose pliers to squeeze down each loop so that the wire is folded back against itself.

⑤ Place one pin on your bench block with the folded end facing away from you.

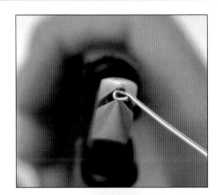

⑥ Use a chasing hammer to tap the folded end of the pin with a motion that is moving away from you. The face of the hammer should be angled slightly downward. This will flatten the pin's head more at its tip than at its base.

⑦ Repeat Steps 4–6 for each length of wire that you prepared in Step 1.

CONTINUED ON NEXT PAGE

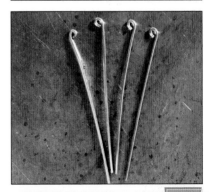

PADDLE HEAD PINS

Paddle head pins are easy to make and have a more artistic look than simple head pins.

1. Prepare each length of wire for your pins as you did for Steps 1–2 of "Simple Head Pins" on p. 50; however, this time, make each one about ⅛ inch longer than you'd like the straight part of the finished pin to be.

2. Place one wire on your bench block, with the end that will be the head pointing away from you.

3. Holding your chasing hammer at a slight downward angle, hammer the end with a motion that is moving away from you and toward the end of the pin.

4. Continue hammering until you have created a small paddle at the end of the wire.

5. Use a needle file to smooth the paddle edges.

6. Repeat Steps 2–5 for each length of wire that you prepared in Step 1.

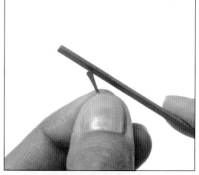

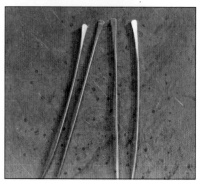

SPIRAL HEAD PINS

These head pins have hammered spirals at the ends.

1. Prepare a length of wire for each pin that you'd like to make, as you did in Steps 1–2 of "Simple Head Pins" on p. 50; however, this time, make each wire about ¾ inch longer than you'd like the straight part of each pin to be.

2. To begin the first pin, use the tips of round nose pliers to create a tiny loop at the end.

3. Optionally, use chain nose pliers or flat nose pliers to flatten down this loop.

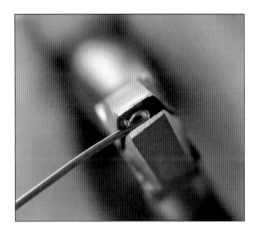

4. With the loop or fold facing away from you and your thumb against the wire at the base of the loop, use flat nose pliers to hold the looped or folded tip flat.

5. Rotate the handle of your pliers away from you while pressing the wire against your thumb to begin a flat spiral.

6. Return the flat nose pliers to their starting position on the new spiral.

7. Repeat Steps 5–6 until you have completed two full coils of spiral.

CONTINUED ON NEXT PAGE

⑧ Use the flat nose pliers to grasp the wire at the base of the spiral, exactly as shown.

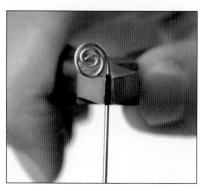

⑨ Use your index finger to bend the spiral slightly toward you to center it on the pin.

⑩ Repeat Steps 2–9 to complete each head pin.

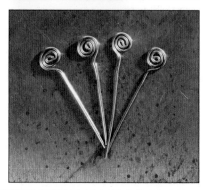

Eye pins are especially easy to make in exactly the lengths you need, and with your choice of eye size. As always, refer to the chart on p. 196–197 for wire gauge recommendations.

SIMPLE EYE PINS

1 Prepare each length of wire as you did for Steps 1–2 of "Paddle Head Pins" on p. 52.

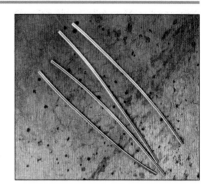

2 To make the eye of each pin, hold one end of the wire with round nose pliers, and rotate your wrist to roll the wire away from you.

3 Return the pliers to their starting position.

CONTINUED ON NEXT PAGE

④ Roll the wire away from you again to complete the eye.

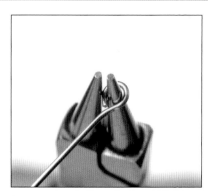

⑤ Return the pliers to their starting position, and use them to hold the wire securely.

⑥ Place the tip of your thumb just below the base of the eye loop, and rotate your wrist slightly back toward you to center the eye on the pin.

⑦ Optionally, hammer the upper edge of the eye using the same hammering technique you would use to hammer a jump ring (see p. 49).

⑧ Repeat Steps 2–7 to complete each simple eye pin.

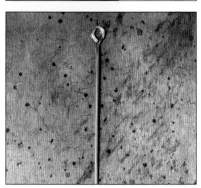

WRAPPED EYE PINS

Wrapped eye pins cannot accidentally be pulled open because the bases of their loops, or eyes, are wrapped closed.

1. Use side cutters to cut a length of wire for each eye pin that you'd like to make. Each should be at least 1¼ inch longer than you'd like the straight part of the finished pin to be.

2. Grasp the wire with round nose pliers about 1 inch from one end of the wire.

3. Use your finger to bend the longer length of wire over the pliers and away from you, and then all the way back toward you again, to create a loop.

4. Switching to flat nose pliers, hold the loop between the jaws of the pliers using your non-dominant hand.

5. Position the loop so that the short tail of wire is pointing up and passing in front of the base of the loop (not behind it).

6. Using your dominant hand, grasp the end of the short tail of wire with round nose pliers, and bend it slowly away from you, over the wire at the base of the loop.

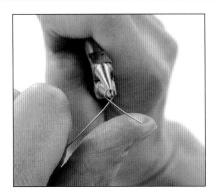

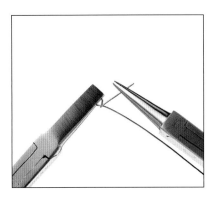

You can use either round nose pliers or chain nose pliers to grip the wire when making wraps. Experiment with both to see which you find more comfortable and less likely to mar your wire.

CONTINUED ON NEXT PAGE

7. Release the wire and reposition the pliers so that you can grasp it again from below the loop, and pull it upward and toward you to complete one wrap.

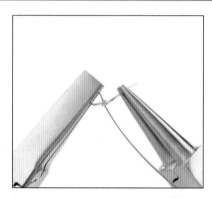

8. Repeat Steps 6–7 to create a total of three or four wraps.

9. Use side cutters to trim off the excess wire as close to the wraps as possible, making a flush cut.

10. Flatten the end of the wire that you just trimmed by squeezing it down with chain nose pliers.

11. Repeat Steps 1–10 to complete each wrapped eye pin.

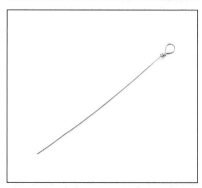

Create
Wire-and-Bead Drops

You can use wire-and-bead drops to embellish almost any type of jewelry. Keep in mind that the recommended wire lengths in these tasks are estimates. You'll need to experiment to find which precise lengths work best for you.

SIMPLE DROPS

① Begin with a head pin whose straight portion is about ¼ inch to ⅜ inch longer than your bead.

② String the bead onto the head pin.

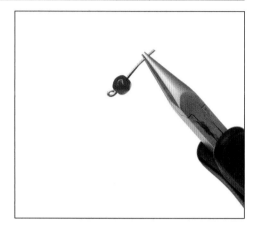

③ Holding the pin in place, bend the wire tail back toward you and against the bead as shown.

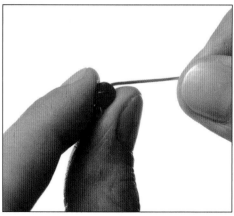

CONTINUED ON NEXT PAGE

④ Grasp the end of the wire with round nose pliers, and rotate your wrist away from you to create a loop.

⑤ If necessary, return the pliers to their starting position, and roll the wire again to complete the entire loop.

Note: *If you use an eye pin instead of a head pin for your drop, you can add a charm or another drop to the bottom by attaching it to the eye loop.*

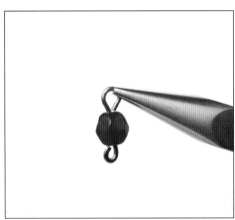

WRAPPED BEAD DROPS

If you wrap the wire at the base of your loop, it cannot be pulled open accidentally.

1. Begin with a head pin whose straight portion is at least 2 inches longer than your bead.

2. String the bead onto the head pin.

3. Use round nose pliers to grasp the wire up against the bead as shown.

4. Bend the rest of the wire back toward you as you did in Step 3 of "Simple Drops" on p. 59.

5. Reposition the round nose pliers so that they grasp the wire just above the bend that you made in Step 4.

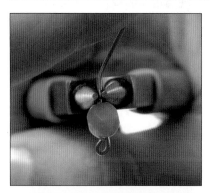

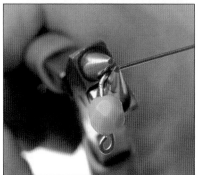

6. Bend the rest of the wire tail away from you, over the nose of the pliers, and all the way around the pliers to form a loop.

7. Remove the round nose pliers.

CONTINUED ON NEXT PAGE

8 Turn the wire over so that the tail is pointing upward.

9 Use chain nose or flat nose pliers to gently hold the loop closed and flat.

10 Using the round nose (or chain nose) pliers in your other hand, grasp the wire tail, and wrap it all the way around the base of the wire just below the loop. You should be wrapping in a direction that is moving away from you.

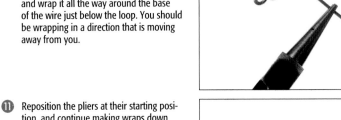

11 Reposition the pliers at their starting position, and continue making wraps down the base of the wire until it is completely covered with wraps.

12 Use side cutters to trim the extra wire tail flush against the wraps.

13 If necessary, squeeze the end of the wire flat with chain nose pliers.

CAGED BEAD DROPS

To create a *caged bead drop*, you wrap wire around the entire bead, not just the loop. Caging works best on round or round-edged beads.

1 Begin with an extra-long wrapped eye pin (p. 57). The exact length of pin you need will depend on the size of your bead and the number of wraps that you'd like to make around it.

2 String the bead onto the eye pin.

3 While holding the bead against the base of the wrapped loop, use your fingers to bend the wire to a 90-degree angle.

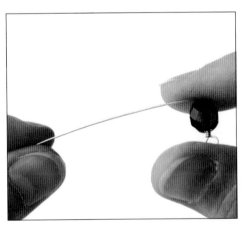

CONTINUED ON NEXT PAGE

④ Use the fingers and thumb of your non-dominant hand to press the wire against the bead at the base of the bead.

⑤ Use the thumb of your dominant hand to push the wire upward against the side of the bead.

⑥ Use your non-dominant hand to slowly turn the bead, while using your other hand to press the wire against the bead, slowly creating wraps.

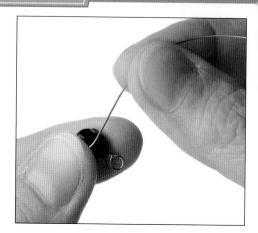

⑦ Create at least one full wrap around the bead. (The number of wraps you make will depend on personal preference and the length of your bead.)

⑧ Using your non-dominant hand, grasp the eye of the wrapped head pin with flat nose pliers.

⑨ Use the fingers of your dominant hand (or round nose pliers) to wrap the wire over and around the eye-pin wraps two or three times.

⑩ Use side cutters to trim off the excess wire as close to the wraps as possible.

⑪ If necessary, use chain nose pliers to squeeze down the tip of the wire you just trimmed.

TIP

You can use either straight or curved chain nose pliers to squeeze down the ends of wire wraps. Curved, or bent nose, pliers often work best because they allow you to hold the pliers at a comfortable angle, and their tips are very narrow for added precision.

You can create necklaces, bracelets, anklets, and long earrings by connecting individual wire-and-bead links.

SIMPLE LINKS

To make a simple bead link, combine the techniques for making a simple eye pin and a wire-and-bead drop.

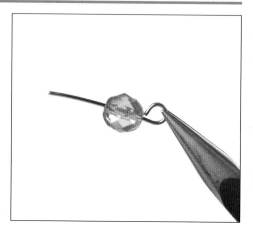

1. Begin with a flush-cut length of wire that is about ½ inch longer than your bead.

2. Use round nose pliers to create a loop at one end as if you were making an eye pin.

3. Place the bead onto the wire and position it against the new loop.

4. Holding the bead in place, perform Steps 3–5 of "Simple Drops" on p. 59–60 to complete the link.

   Note: Links tend to look best if the loops face opposite directions.

WRAPPED BEAD LINKS

To make a wrapped bead link, combine the techniques for making a wrapped eye pin and a wire-and-bead drop.

1. Begin with a wrapped eye pin (see p. 57) whose straight portion is at least 4 inches longer than your bead.

2. Place the bead on the wire, and position it up against the first wrapped loop.

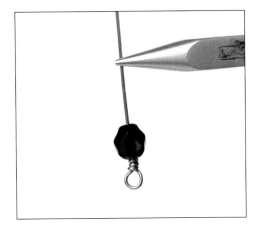

3. Perform Steps 3–13 of "Wrapped Bead Drops" on p. 61–63 to complete the second wrapped loop.

CONTINUED ON NEXT PAGE

CAGED BEAD LINKS

You can make caged bead links
by combining the techniques
for making caged bead drops
and wrapped bead links.

1 Make a wrapped bead link using
a much longer piece of wire than
you would normally use (at least
10 times longer than your bead),
but do *not* trim off the extra wire
after the final wrap.

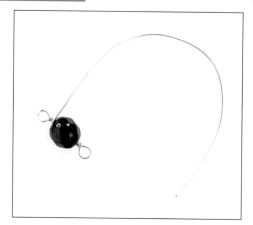

2 Hold the second wrapped loop
and the end of the bead using
the fingers and thumb of your
non-dominant hand.

3 Use your dominant hand to
slowly wrap the wire around the
bead toward the eye of the head
pin, turning the bead with your
non-dominant hand as you make
wraps.

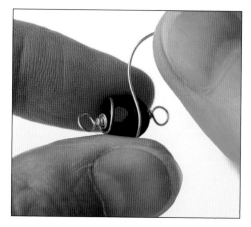

4 When you reach the wraps on the eye pin, wrap the wire around them two or three times, as you would to complete a caged bead drop.

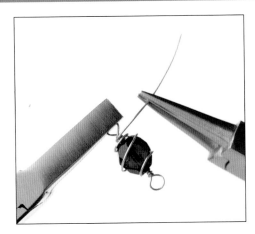

5 Use side cutters to trim off the excess wire.

6 If necessary, use chain nose pliers to squeeze down the tip of the wire that you just trimmed.

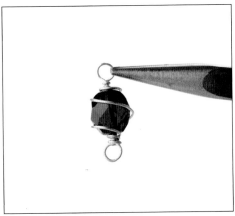

Connect Wire-and-Bead Links

You can connect wire-and-bead links to one another to create a beaded chain, or connect them to lengths of pre-made chain to serve as beaded accents.

CONNECT LINKS WITH JUMP RINGS

You can connect simple and wrapped links to one another using jump rings. Simply open a jump ring, slip on the end-loops of two links, and then close the jump ring.

To ensure that the links won't come apart, you need to use larger-gauge wire (like 18 gauge), and/or wire with a harder temper than dead-soft. Alternatively, you can make link connections stronger by using two jump rings side-by-side in between links, instead of one.

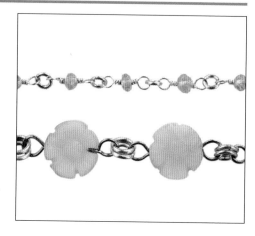

CONNECT SIMPLE LINKS

Connect simple links by opening and closing their loops around one another.

① Open one loop on a simple bead link by using chain nose pliers to twist the open half to the side.

② Insert the closed loop of another bead link into the open loop on the first.

③ Use the chain nose pliers to bend the open loop back into its closed position.

Some connected simple bead links are shown here.

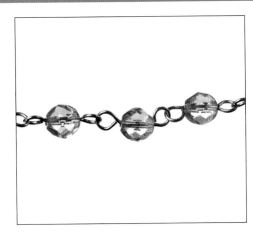

CONNECT WRAPPED LINKS

Because the loops on wrapped links (including caged links) do not open, you need to connect them one-by-one as you make them.

① Complete Steps 1–2 of "Wrapped Bead Links" on p. 67. You now have a link with the first side looped and wrapped, and the bead is in place.

② Grasp the wire tail at the end of the bead using round nose pliers, with the tail pointing upward.

③ Bend the wire tail back toward you.

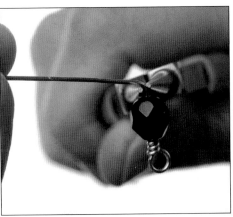

CONTINUED ON NEXT PAGE

④ Reposition the round nose pliers to grasp the wire just above the bend that you made in Step 3.

⑤ Use your fingers to wrap the wire tail away from you and over the pliers to create a full loop.

⑥ Remove the pliers and slip the completed loop of another bead link over the wire tail and into the loop.

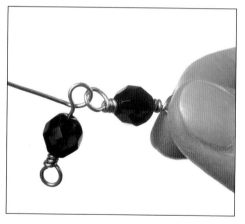

7 Grasp the unfinished loop with chain nose pliers, being careful not to mar the other loop that is now inside.

8 Use the round nose pliers to wrap the wire tail around the base of the wire.

9 Complete this wrap as usual.

Some completed wrapped bead links are shown here.

TIP

You can connect links to lengths of pre-made chain by using the first and last links in the chain in place of bead links. To cut bulk chain when its loops are soldered closed, use side cutters to cut through and remove a link. To make a length of chain the same length as a previous one, hang the previous length and the uncut chain on a straight pin, hold up the pin so that the chains are aligned, and trim the uncut chain to match the previous length.

Make Basic Wire Clasps

You can make your own basic clasps by forming clasp eyes and hooks with wire. As always, keep in mind that the recommended wire lengths in these tasks are estimates. Refer to the chart on p. 196–197 for wire gauge recommendations.

SIMPLE CLASP EYE

The part of a clasp where your hook attaches is called the *clasp eye*. It can simply be a large jump ring, but a figure-eight style eye is more substantial and easier to use.

1. Beginning with a flush-cut length of wire about 1¼ inches long, use the largest part of your round nose pliers to create a large loop at one end.

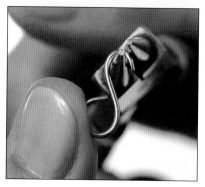

2. Turn the piece around, and create a smaller loop at the other end that faces in the opposite direction to the first loop.

3. Place the clasp eye on a bench block with the large loop pointing away from you.

4. Hammering away from you, slightly flatten the top of the large loop.

5. Turn the piece around on the bench block and repeat Step 4 on the smaller loop.

6. Use flat nose pliers to wiggle both loops closed as needed.

A completed simple clasp eye is shown here, with a hook attached.

WRAPPED CLASP EYE

1. Beginning with a flush-cut length of wire about 5 inches long, grasp the wire with the largest part of your round nose pliers, about 1½ inches from one end.

2. Bend the shorter (1½-inch) end of the wire away from you over the pliers to create a full loop.

CONTINUED ON NEXT PAGE

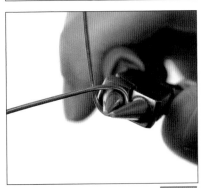

③ Remove the round nose pliers, and grasp the loop with flat nose pliers.

④ Use the round nose pliers to wrap the tail two or three times below the loop.

⑤ Trim off the excess wire.

⑥ Turn the piece around, and grasp the wrap with the round nose pliers.

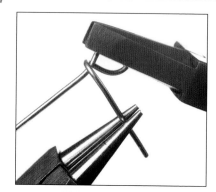

⑦ Bend the unlooped end of the wire toward you, creating a bend next to the wraps.

⑧ Use the round nose pliers to grasp the wire just above the bend.

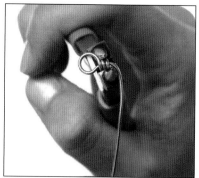

⑨ Use your fingers to bend the wire away from you and over the round nose pliers. This creates another loop that is smaller than the first.

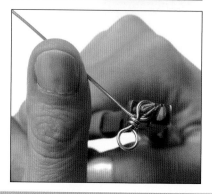

10 Holding the loop with flat nose pliers, use the round nose pliers to wrap the remaining wire end around the first wrap two or three times.

11 Trim off the excess wire tail and gently squeeze down the end with flat nose pliers.

12 If necessary, file the wire end with a needle file to smooth its edges.

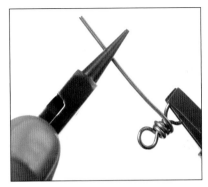

A finished wrapped clasp eye is shown here, with a hook attached.

CONTINUED ON NEXT PAGE

TIP

Notice that wrapped clasp eyes are really just wire links without beads. You can also use simple, wrapped, and caged bead links as clasp eyes. Just make one loop large enough for your hook to pass through.

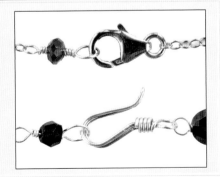

SIMPLE HOOK

1 Begin with a flush-cut piece of wire that is about 1¾ to 2 inches long.

2 Using the tips of the round nose pliers, roll one end of the wire into a small loop.

3 Grasp the wire about ⅛ inch away from the base of the small loop, using the largest part of the round nose pliers.

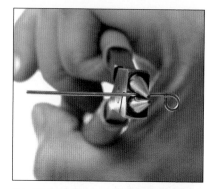

4 Rotate your wrist away from you to roll the wire upward into a large loop shape.

5 Turn the piece around and use the tips of the round nose pliers to grasp the other end of the wire.

6 Roll that end away from you to create a smaller loop.

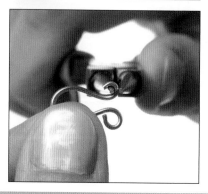

7. Place the hook on a bench block with the large hook-loop facing away from you.

8. Hammering away from you, slightly flatten the top curved portion of the hook.

9. Use your fingers to wiggle the hook so that it is just slightly open (if it's not already).

10. If needed, use flat nose pliers to wiggle the small loop at the other end closed.

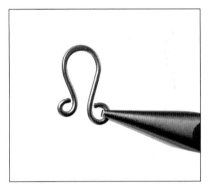

CONTINUED ON NEXT PAGE

SPIRAL HOOK

1. Using wire directly from the spool and flush cut at the end, use round nose pliers to create a small loop.

2. Grasp the loop with flat nose pliers, and place your thumb against the wire at the base of the loop.

3. To begin a flat spiral, rotate the handle of your pliers away from you while pressing the wire against your thumb.

4. Continue this process to create two or three flat spirals.

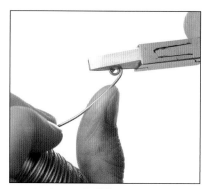

5. Grasp the wire at the base of the spiral with the tips of the round nose pliers.

6. Without removing the round nose pliers, use your fingers to complete an additional half-flat spiral.

7. Use side cutters to flush cut the wire about 1¼ inches away from the flat spiral.

8. With the flat spiral facing toward you, grasp the tip of the wire with the round nose pliers.

9. Roll the pliers away from you to create a small loop.

10 Turn the piece around so that the flat spiral is facing toward you.

11 Grasp the wire just beneath the loop you made in Step 9, using the largest part of the round nose pliers.

12 Roll the round nose pliers away from you to create the large hook loop.

13 Use your fingers to wiggle the hook slightly open and into alignment with the flat-spiraled base of the hook.

14 Place the piece on a bench block with the hook loop pointing away from you.

15 Hammering away from you, slightly flatten the top of the hook.

16 Turn the piece around on the bench block, and hammer away from you to slightly flatten the bottom of the flat spiral.

CONTINUED ON NEXT PAGE

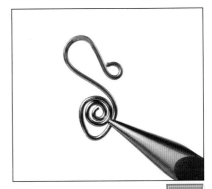

"S" HOOK

As its name implies, an "S" hook is shaped like the letter S.

1. Begin with a flush-cut piece of wire that is about 2½ inches in length.

2. Use round nose pliers to create a small loop at one end.

3. Turn the wire over, and create a small loop at the other end, facing the opposite direction.

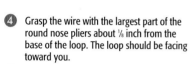

4. Grasp the wire with the largest part of the round nose pliers about ⅛ inch from the base of the loop. The loop should be facing toward you.

5. Rotate the pliers away from you to create a complete large loop. The small loop should touch the center of the wire.

6. Turn the piece around and repeat Steps 4–5 to create a matching large loop on the other end, facing the opposite direction.

7. Place the hook on a bench block.

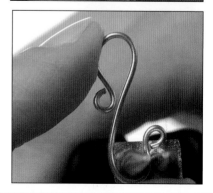

8 Hammering away from you, slightly flatten the top curved portion of one of the large loops.

9 Turn the piece around on the bench block, and hammer the other end.

10 Use your fingers or flat nose pliers to wiggle one loop open a little.

11 Wiggle the other loop completely closed (if it isn't already).

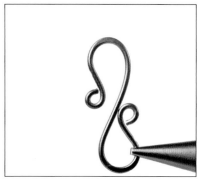

You can use a mandrel to create sets of matching ear wires for your earrings. To review the technique for making ear wires using a jig, see Chapter 7.

BASIC FRENCH HOOKS

This example uses a 5/16-inch wood dowel as a mandrel. You can experiment with other dowel sizes, and different lengths of wire, to make larger or smaller hooks.

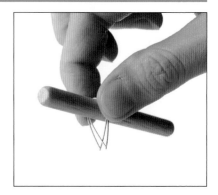

1. Begin with two 1¾- to 2-inch lengths of 20- or 22-gauge wire. For best results, use wire with half-hard temper.

2. Hold both wires against the dowel, centered so that an equal length of wire extends on both sides.

3. Use your fingers to bend down both ends of each wire until they just cross below the mandrel.

4. Slide the wires off of the mandrel.

5. Use round nose pliers to create a loop at one end of each wire, with the loop facing away from the opposite end of the wire.

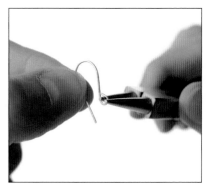

6. Grasp the opposite end of each wire with the thickest part of the jaws of round nose pliers, and roll the pliers to create a gentle, outward curve at each end.

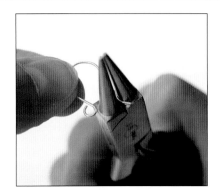

7. Place the hooks on a bench block, and use a chasing hammer to slightly flatten the upper curve of each hook, using the same technique you would use to hammer a simple clasp hook (see p. 78–79).

8. Use your fingers to gently bend each hook, as necessary, into the desired shape, making sure that the hooks match one another.

9. Use a needle file to smooth the curved end of each hook. Be sure to remove all jagged edges.

A pair of French hooks are shown here.

CONTINUED ON NEXT PAGE

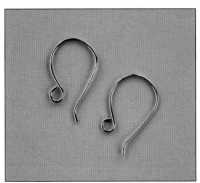

BASIC HOOPS

You can also create basic hoops using a mandrel. They can be worn plain, or with charms or drops.

1. Begin with two lengths of 20- or 22-gauge half-hard wire that are each about ½ inch longer than you would like the circumference of the hoops to be.

2. Use round nose pliers to convert each wire into a simple eye pin (see p. 55).

3. Use a bench block and chasing hammer to slightly flatten the tops of both pin eyes. (If the eye loops open up during hammering, use chain nose pliers to wiggle them closed.)

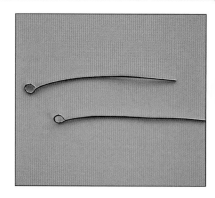

4. Press the eye of one pin against a mandrel using the thumb of your dominant hand.

5. Use the thumb and fingers of your other hand to wrap the wire tightly all the way around the mandrel.

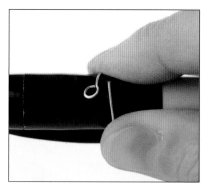

6. Pass the end of the wire through the pin eye.

7. Grasp the wire-end with round nose pliers and bend the wire back in the opposite direction. The wire should now be snugly secured around the mandrel.

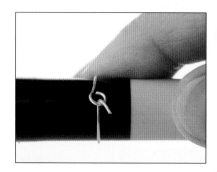

8. Slide the loop off of the mandrel and place it on a bench block, with the pin eye over the edge of the bench block so that the loop lies flat, as shown.

9. Lightly hammer the loop, all the way around, to slightly flatten and stiffen it.

10. If needed, slide the loop back onto the mandrel to restore its circular shape.

11. Trim the bent wire end to about ⅛ inch in length.

12. Use a needle file to smooth all of the rough edges on the wire end.

13. Repeat Steps 4–12 to complete the other hoop.

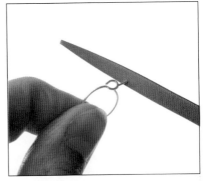

To unfasten a hoop, gently pull the wire-end out of the wire loop.

chapter 5

More Advanced Techniques

This chapter covers many of the more advanced techniques used by wire jewelry artists and designers. Don't be afraid to experiment by altering the examples to suit your taste. Over time, you'll develop your own unique preferences and personal style. Because many of these tasks require practice, be sure to use inexpensive wire the first time you try them.

Make a Wrapped Briolette Drop

Briolettes are drop-shaped beads that have elegant, triangular or diamond-shaped facets. They're commonly used as focal beads and centerpieces and are some of the most popular beads to wrap with wire.

BASIC WRAPPED BRIOLETTE

Use this technique to create a wrapped loop at the top of a briolette.

① Using 26- or 24-gauge wire directly from the spool or coil, insert the end of the wire through the hole in the briolette until a tail of at least ½ inch of wire protrudes from the other side.

② While holding the briolette in place, bend the wire on the spool-end of the briolette toward the top of the briolette.

③ On the other side of the briolette, bend the wire tail in the same manner. The wire is now crossed just above the top of the briolette.

④ Using flat nose pliers, grasp the shorter wire, just above the very top of the briolette.

⑤ Bend the wire directly upward.

⑥ Turn the briolette around and repeat Steps 4–5 with the wire on the other side.

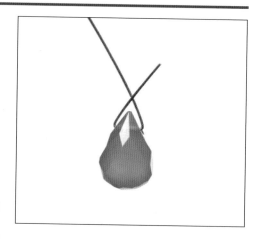

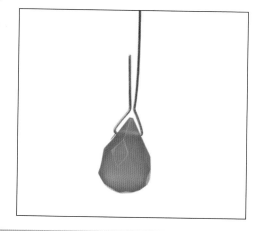

7 Using sharp side cutters, carefully trim the wire tail about ⅛ inch above the bend that you made in the shorter wire.

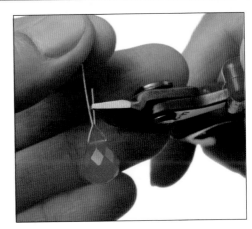

8 With the tips of chain nose pliers, grasp the two wires, side-by-side.

9 Align the upper edge of the pliers with the end of the short wire.

10 Use your other hand to bend the spool-end of the wire downward to one side.

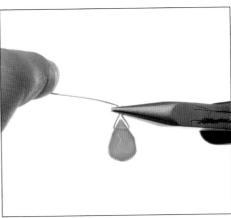

CONTINUED ON NEXT PAGE

⑪ Grasp the spool-end of the wire with round nose pliers just above the bend that you made in Step 10.

⑫ Using your other hand, wrap the wire around the nose of the pliers to create a loop.

⑬ While still holding the loop with the round nose pliers, wrap the spool-end of the wire around both wires below the loop.

⑭ Continue wrapping until you reach the bends in the wires.

15 Trim the wire with side cutters.

16 If necessary, use chain nose pliers to squeeze down the end of the wire.

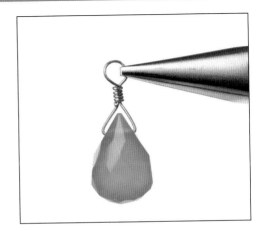

WRAPPED BRIOLETTE CAP

This method creates a double-wire loop and a "cap" of wrapped wire that hides the top of the briolette.

1 Begin with a length of 26- or 24-gauge wire that is about 10–12 inches long. (Smaller briolettes may require a little less, and larger ones may require a little more.)

2 Insert the wire through the hole in the briolette, and center the briolette along the wire.

3 Bend both ends of the wire upward until they cross.

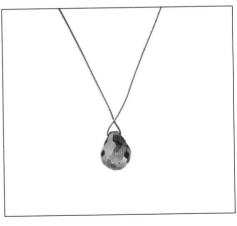

CONTINUED ON NEXT PAGE

④ Use your fingers to squeeze the wires together just past the tip of the briolette.

⑤ Pull the wires through your fingers to straighten them, beginning at the point just above the small bends you made in Step 4.

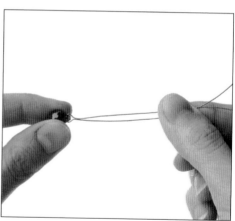

6 Grasp both wires with round nose pliers, just past the tip of the briolette.

7 Bend both wires to one side, and then wrap them completely around the round nose pliers to create a loop.

8 Wrap both wires around the base of the loop, taking care to keep them parallel to one another (do not allow them to cross one another).

9 Continue wrapping past the top of the briolette, until you have your desired size of "cap."

CONTINUED ON NEXT PAGE

⑩ Trim one of the wires close to the wraps and use chain nose pliers (or your fingernail) to tuck it up under the lowermost wraps.

⑪ Wrap the other wire around the briolette a little more, and then trim and tuck it under the wraps.

A completed wrapped briolette cap is shown here

TIP

If you'd prefer to have a single-wire loop at the top of your briolette cap, you can make a basic wrapped loop and then continue wrapping down the sides of the briolette. However, the double-wire method is faster and usually results in more evenly-shaped caps.

Twist Wire

You can use twisted wire in place of regular wire to make more ornate and interesting jewelry components. Square wire can be twisted using a single strand, and round wire is usually twisted in double strands. To avoid breakage, only twist wire that has dead-soft temper. (To review wire temper, see p. 12 in Chapter 1.)

TWISTED SQUARE WIRE

The easiest way to twist square wire is with a pin vice. (For more information on pin vices, see p. 29 in Chapter 2.)

1. Beginning with a length of 20-gauge or smaller square wire (or wire directly from the spool), secure the very end of the wire in the jaws of the pin vice.

2. With your non-dominant hand, use taped flat nose pliers to grasp the wire about 1½ inches away from the pin vice.

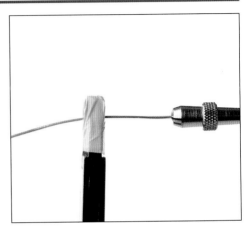

3. With your dominant hand, slowly turn the pin vice, making sure that the vice stays in its fully locked-down position to keep the wire from slipping.

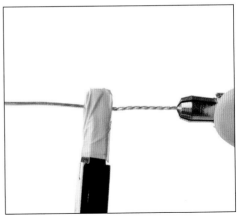

CONTINUED ON NEXT PAGE

④ When you reach your desired density of twists (no more than about five or six full twists), release the pin vice so that it is in its fully open position.

⑤ Release the flat nose pliers and slide the wire into and through the pin vice until the place where the twists begin is positioned in the jaws of the vice. (If your vice has a cap on its end, remove it so that the wire can pass all the way through.)

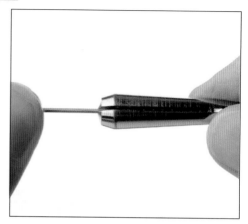

⑥ Lock-down the jaws of the pin vice to re-secure the wire.

⑦ Repeat Steps 2–4 until you have your desired length of twisted wire.

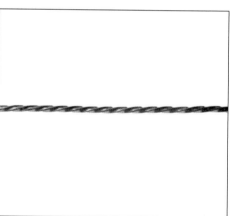

DOUBLE-TWISTED ROUND WIRE

You can use an inexpensive hand drill and some utility hooks to twist together two strands of round wire.

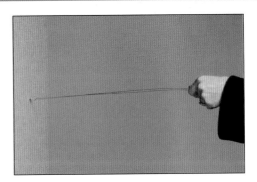

1 Beginning with a length of 20-gauge wire about 3 feet long, insert the wire into a utility eye hook that is securely attached to your workbench or another heavy, stable object.

2 Center the eye hook along the wire, and pull both ends of the wire together.

3 Hold the wire securely with your fingers an inch or two from the ends, and use chain nose pliers to twist the ends together several times.

TIP

Is your wire breaking when you make twists? This will happen if you are twisting too tightly (that is, making too many twists), or if the temper of your wire was too high when you began twisting. Always twist dead-soft (not half-hard or hard) wire that has not been hammered or repeatedly straightened, and be careful not to over-twist.

CONTINUED ON NEXT PAGE

④ Insert a small hook (a cup hook is used in the example) into the chuck of a hand drill, and tighten the chuck securely over the screw-end of the hook.

⑤ Slide the twisted end of the wire over the hook in the drill.

⑥ Gently pull the wire taut between the eye hook and the drill hook.

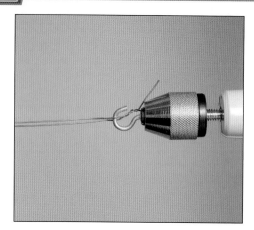

⑦ Slowly turn the crank on the hand drill to begin twisting the two strands of wire together.

⑧ As the wire becomes shorter, walk toward the eye hook, keeping the wire taut as you work.

⑨ Continue twisting until you have the desired density of twists along the wire.

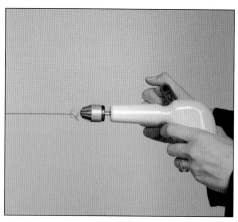

10 Trim both ends of the twisted wire with side cutters to prepare it for use.

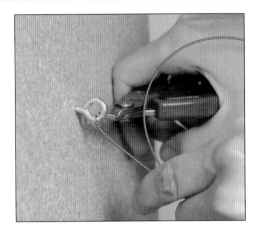

OTHER DOUBLE-TWISTING METHODS

If you do not have a hand drill, try twisting your wire with a pencil, pen, or wooden dowel. Insert it behind the twisted-together wire ends, and turn it repeatedly to create the twist. This technique is more time-consuming than using a hand drill, but it also works.

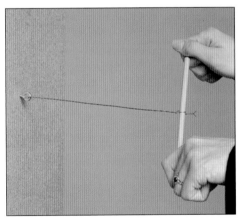

CONTINUED ON NEXT PAGE

Some jewelry making suppliers sell a specialized tool for twisting wire. It looks like a bulky pair of pliers. You can lock the ends of your wire into its jaws, and then pull a lever at the other end of the tool to cause it to spin. This tool may speed up your wire twisting, but it's a little awkward and uncomfortable to use. Try one before purchasing it to see whether it's right for you.

TIP

Make Consistent Twists

The density of twists in your wire depends on how tightly the wire is twisted. More loosely twisted wire has fewer twists than more tightly twisted wire, and vice versa. One way to make consistent twists with multiple lengths of wire is to keep track of the number of twists-per-inch that you would like to make. As you twist your wire, occasionally stop and use a ruler to count the twists-per-inch. Stop twisting when you reach your desired density of twists.

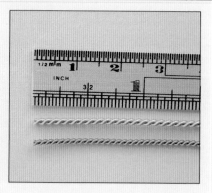

Use
Coiled Wraps

You can make plain wire look more detailed by wrapping it with tight coils of smaller-gauge wire.

BASIC COILING TECHNIQUE

1 Create a jewelry component that you would like to wrap with coils. (The example is a wrapped clasp eye made with 18-gauge wire.)

2 Cut a length of 24-gauge or smaller wire, using the chart on p. 196–197 as a guide.

3 Use flat nose pliers to fold-over about 1 inch of the wire, as shown. This will be the "wire tail."

4 Slip the folded wire over the portion of the component that you would like to wrap with coils.

5 Using the fingers of your non-dominant hand, press the wire tail against the component in a place where you will not be wrapping coils. (This creates leverage for making the wraps.)

CONTINUED ON NEXT PAGE

⑥ With your dominant hand, slowly begin wrapping the wire all the way around the component wire, using your index finger to guide the coil so that it lies flat.

⑦ If your component has a closed loop, like the example, pass the wire through the inside of the loop, and then pull it out again, to make each wrap. The wire will bend a little, but try to keep it from kinking.

⑧ As you make wraps, occasionally use your fingernail to press the new coils flat against the previous coils.

⑨ When the wire becomes too short to continue wrapping using your fingers, use round nose or chain nose pliers to wrap it instead.

⑩ When you have finished making coils, use side cutters to trim the wire as close to the coils as possible.

⑪ Use chain nose pliers to squeeze down the very end of the wire.

⑫ Go back to the beginning of the wire, trim off the wire tail, and use chain nose pliers to squeeze down its end.

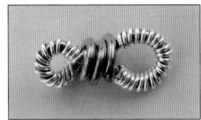

TIP

When you create coils on smaller components, like the clasp eye shown in the example, your wire is more likely to become brittle and break as you make wraps. If you find this happening, take these steps:

- Try using smaller-gauge wire.
- Make sure you are using unused, dead-soft wire.
- Work slowly, and do your best to keep the wire from kinking as you make wraps.
- Make sure your wire is long enough to allow you to make smooth wraps. If the wire becomes very short, it will be more likely to kink and break.
- If you still have trouble, try creating the coils before you finish making the component (see "Coil an Unfinished Component" on the next page).

CONTINUED ON NEXT PAGE

COIL AN UNFINISHED COMPONENT

For some components, like the "S" hook used in this example, you may find it easier to make the coils before completing all of the steps for making the component.

① Perform any initial steps for creating your component that will result in features that you do not intend to wrap. For example, to begin an "S" hook, complete Steps 1–3 on p. 82.

② Cut a length of 24-gauge or smaller wire, using the chart on p. 196–197 as a guide. (In the example, about 2 inches of the "S" hook will be wrapped.)

③ Perform Steps 3–11 of "Basic Coiling Technique" to wrap the entire straight portion of the component-wire, end-to-end. (You should be able to wrap this straight wire faster than you would a closed-loop component.)

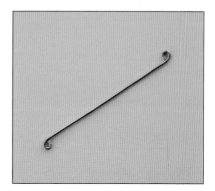

④ Now perform all of the steps to complete the component, *except* for any steps that normally require hammering on the portion(s) you have wrapped with coils. (Hammering can damage wrapped coils, so it's best to avoid it.)

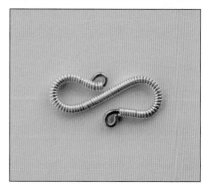

DOUBLE-WRAPPED WIRE BEADS

You can make chunky beads by wrapping a coil of wire around bare wire. Once you learn the basic method, try experimenting with different lengths of wire and different mandrel sizes.

1. Following the directions for making a wire coil on a mandrel (see p. 45 in Chapter 4), use a small mandrel and 20-gauge wire to create a wire coil 2–3 inches long.

2. After removing the coil from the mandrel and trimming the ends, insert a 7- to 8-inch length of 18-gauge wire all the way through the coil.

3. Position the coil at the center of the 18-gauge wire. (Alternatively, for smaller coils, wrap coils of 24-gauge or smaller wire directly onto the 18-gauge wire rather than making them separately on a mandrel.)

4. Keeping the coil in this position, press one end of the coil firmly against the mandrel.

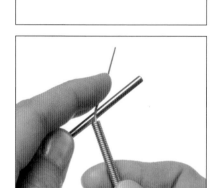

5. Slowly turn the mandrel while pressing the coil against it to create a new coil moving in the opposite direction. In effect, you are wrapping the 18-gauge wire around the mandrel and taking the 20-gauge (or 24-gauge) coil along with it.

CONTINUED ON NEXT PAGE

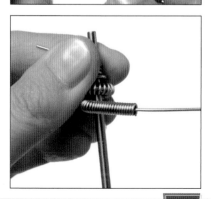

6 Continue coiling until you reach the end of the 18-gauge wire.

7 Turn the mandrel around and coil the other end of the 18-gauge wire around the mandrel.

8 Slide the wire off of the mandrel and trim the ends, making flush cuts.

A completed double-wrapped bead is shown here.

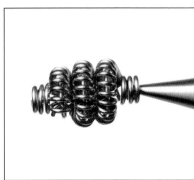

Specialty Wire Coiling Tools

If you have trouble neatly coiling a long length of wire on a regular mandrel, try using a specialty wire-coiling tool instead (as shown in the photo on the right). There are several styles to choose from. Most include a mandrel attachment with a handle or crank for easy turning, and a notch or other mechanism for securing your wire. Some are even designed to help you make double-wrapped beads faster and easier than you can using the traditional method.

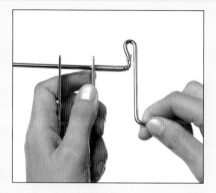

Wrap Beads within a Wire Frame

You can create elaborate pendants and cuff bracelets by wrapping beads and wire onto wirework frames. Begin by shaping a frame using heavy-gauge wire, and then fill it with wrapped-in beads on small-gauge wire.

BASIC PENDANT FRAME

A pendant frame can be just about any shape, but round frames are the easiest to construct. Notice that you wrap the top using the same method that is used to wrap a briolette.

1 Beginning with 18- or 16-gauge wire directly from the spool or coil, wrap the first several inches of wire around a round mandrel that is as large as you would like the inside of your pendant frame to be.

2 Double over the ends of the wire, leaving about 1 inch of wire tail.

3 Hold the wire on the mandrel with one hand, and use your other hand to grasp the base of the wire tail with flat nose pliers.

4 Use the flat nose pliers to bend the wire tail directly upward.

5 Use the pliers to grasp the base of the wire coming around the other side of the mandrel.

6 Bend this wire upward at a 90-degree angle directly next to the bend that you made in Step 4.

7 Remove the frame from the mandrel.

8 Using heavy, sharp side cutters, flush cut the short wire about ⅛ inch above the top of the circle.

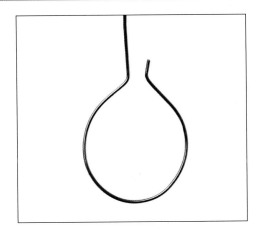

9 Grasp the base of the two wires, just above the wire circle, with chain nose pliers.

10 Align the upper edge of the pliers with the end of the short wire that you cut in Step 8.

11 Use your other hand to bend the spool-end of the wire downward to one side.

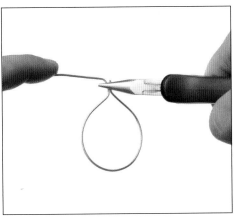

CONTINUED ON NEXT PAGE

⑫ Grasp the spool-end of the wire with round nose pliers, just above the bend that you made in Step 11.

⑬ Using your other hand, wrap the wire around the nose of the pliers to create a loop.

⑭ While still holding the loop with the round nose pliers, slowly wrap the spool-end of the wire snugly around both wires below the loop.

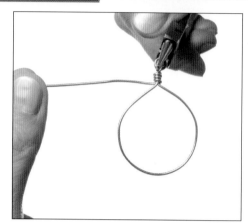

⑮ Continue wrapping until you reach the base of the wires at the top of the circle.

⑯ Make a flush cut to trim off the wire.

⑰ If needed, use chain nose pliers to neaten the coils and squeeze down the wire end.

Note: If your frame has lost its circular shape, slip it back onto the mandrel as far as it will go to reshape it.

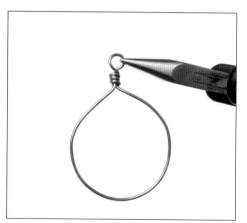

WRAPPING-IN THE BEADS

You can fill your pendant frame with any beads that will fit inside it. Rows of beads can be aligned closely together, or they can zigzag loosely across the frame.

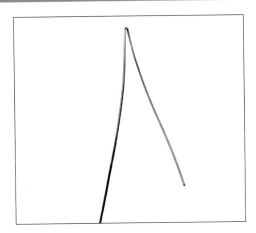

1. Beginning with 3 feet of dead-soft 24-gauge or smaller wire, use chain nose pliers to fold-over about 4 inches of wire at one end.

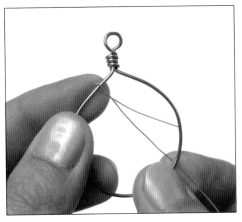

2. Position the wire horizontally over what will be the front of the pendant.

3. Slide one side of the pendant frame all the way into the fold in the wire.

4. Position the wire close to the top of the frame.

5. Using the fingers of one hand, hold the long end of the wire against the opposite side of the frame.

6. With your other hand, use chain nose pliers to bring the short end of the wire up through the frame.

CONTINUED ON NEXT PAGE

7 Securely wrap the short end of the wire around the side of the frame.

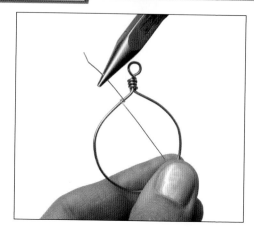

8 Continue wrapping around the side of the frame until you have made five or six wraps. You will have a tail of extra wire remaining after this step. For now, leave it in place to use for leverage.

Note: If the rest of your wire is bent, use nylon jaw pliers now to straighten it. You can stop and straighten the wire after you wrap each row of beads into the frame, if necessary.

9. String on enough beads to make up the first row.

10. Slide the beads up against the side of the frame.

11. Bring the wire down through the frame and under its opposite side.

12. Keeping the wire taut, bring it back up and around the frame.

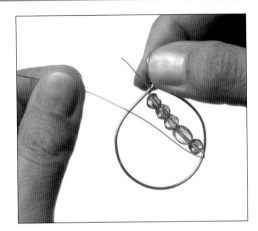

13. Wrap the wire around the frame five or six times in a downward direction.

14. String on the next row of beads.

15. Bring the wire over and around the opposite side of the frame and create five or six more wraps.

16. Continue adding rows of beads until you reach the bottom of the frame.

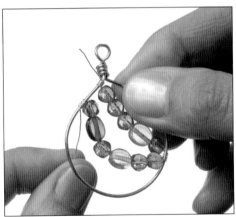

CONTINUED ON NEXT PAGE

⑰ After securing the final row of beads with five or six wraps around the frame, use side cutters to trim the wire flush with the frame at both the top and bottom.

⑱ If needed, squeeze down both ends of the wire using chain nose pliers.

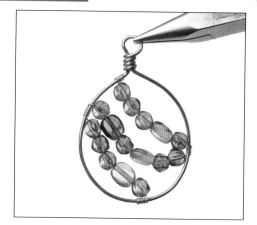

TIP

More Framework Ideas

You can make wire frames in just about any shape. Look around your house for interesting items to use as mandrels. Or, if you're short on time or prefer a more finished appearance, try using pre-made pendant frames. You can often find them at local bead shops or on the Internet. To get even more creative, look for found objects with general frame-like shapes. An example is shown in the photo on the right, where beads are wrapped into a pewter finger ring. See what kind of unusual jewelry designs you can invent by wrapping objects with beads.

BASIC CUFF BRACELET FRAME

Try this basic method for making a simple cuff bracelet frame. You can customize the design by changing the frame's width and shape.

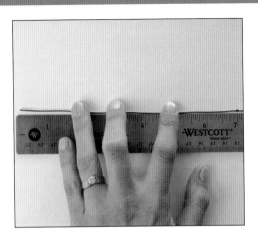

1. Beginning with 14-gauge wire directly from the spool or coil, with the end flush-cut, place the first 8–10 inches of wire along a ruler.

2. With a permanent marker, mark the wire about 7–9 inches from the end (7 inches will make a smaller bracelet, and 9 inches will make a larger one).

   Note: You can remove the mark later using nail polish remover or by lightly filing it off with a needle file.

3. You may use the marker as a mandrel by holding the wire crosswise against it. The ink mark should be centered above the mandrel.

4. Bend both sides of the wire down over the mandrel.

CONTINUED ON NEXT PAGE

5 Using side cutters, flush-cut the spool-end of the wire so that both wire ends are the same length. The wire now has a long "U" shape.

Note: *You can straighten the frame at this point by holding the wire at the base of the "U" and pulling both ends of the wire through nylon jaw pliers.*

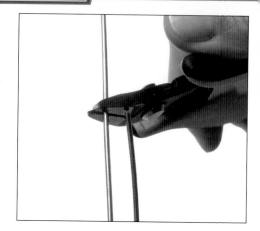

6 Place the frame over a bracelet mandrel or a mandrel substitute, such as a jar or flashlight handle. An eyeglass case is used in the example.

7 Bend down both ends of the frame over the mandrel to form the frame into a curve.

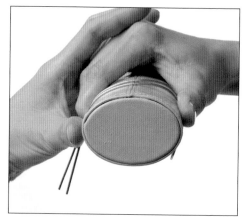

8 After removing the wire from the mandrel, hold the frame with the bottom of the "U" closest to you, and grasp the end of the upper wire with round nose pliers.

9 Roll the pliers away from you to create a loose spiral.

10 Turn the frame over and repeat Steps 8–9 to form a loose spiral on the other wire end.

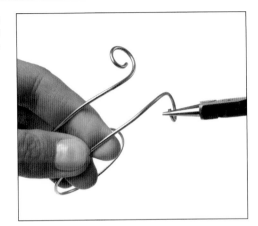

11 Manipulate the wire with your fingers as needed to bring it into an oval cuff-bracelet shape.

Note: You can make the cuff a little larger by gently pulling the ends away from each other, or smaller by bending them closer together.

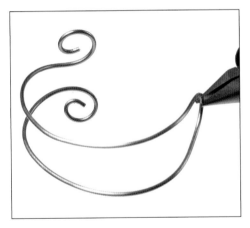

CONTINUED ON NEXT PAGE

WRAPPING-IN THE BEADS

Fill your bracelet with beads using the same general technique that you use for a pendant frame.

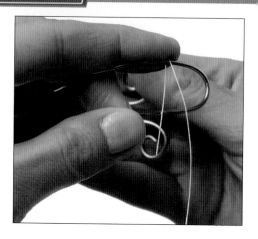

1. Beginning with about 3 feet of dead-soft 24-gauge (or smaller) wire, use chain nose pliers to fold-over 4 inches of wire at one end.

2. Position the wire vertically over the frame near the "U" end of the frame.

3. Slide the top wire of the frame all the way into the fold in the 24-gauge wire.

4. Using the fingers of one hand, hold the long end of the 24-gauge wire against the bottom wire of the frame.

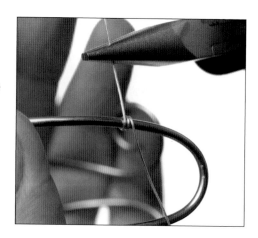

5. With your other hand, use chain nose pliers to bring the shorter wire end up from below the top of the frame and toward the open end of the frame.

6. Use chain nose pliers to wrap the wire around the top of the frame five or six times, moving toward the open end of the frame.

7. String on enough beads to reach the bottom of the frame where you would like the first row of beads to connect.

8. Keeping the beads within the frame, bend the long end of wire over the bottom of the frame.

9. Wrap this wire around the bottom of the frame five or six times.

10. Continue adding beads and wrapping the ends under, then over, the opposite side of the frame until you reach the open end of the frame.

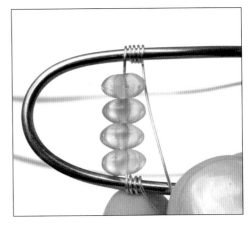

11. After stringing on the beads for the final row, wrap the end of the wire five or six times around the frame.

12. Use side cutters to trim off the excess wire tail at both ends of the frame.

13. If needed, use chain nose pliers to flatten the ends against the frame.

Note: If you use up the length of wire at any time before finishing the bracelet, end the wire by wrapping it five or six times around the frame. Begin a new length of 24-gauge wire by wrapping it around the opposite side of the frame.

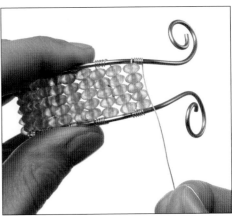

CONTINUED ON NEXT PAGE

A completed bracelet is shown here.

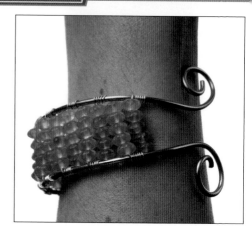

TIP

Use Coils to Join Freeform Elements

You can use the basic coiling technique to join together freeform wire elements within a framework. Begin by coiling around just the frame, and then incorporate a portion of another wire component (like a big wire loop, ring, or loose spiral) into the wraps.

In this example, a freeform loose spiral was wrapped into the frame along with a mix of

beads. In some places, wraps were made on top of previous wraps so that beads could be added to fill-in empty spaces in the design.

Wrap Beads onto a Wire Frame

In addition to wrapping beads between two sides of a frame, you can also wrap them onto the frame itself.

Begin by constructing the wire frame of your choice.

1. If you would like to wrap beads within the frame, do so now.

2. Using a long piece of dead-soft 24-gauge (or smaller) wire (the length will depend on the sizes of your frame and beads), make at least 3 or 4 coils around the frame, with the wire coming out from behind the frame and pointing outward. Do not trim off the wire tail.

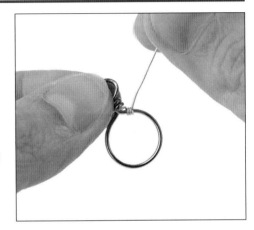

3. String on the first bead that you would like to wrap onto the frame. (Small beads work best.)

4. Position the bead so that it is against and parallel to the frame. You may need to slide the bead over a little on the wire in order to do this. (The side of the bead, not its hole, should be against the frame.)

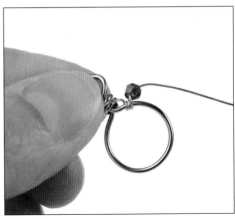

CONTINUED ON NEXT PAGE

5 Using the fingers of your non-dominant hand, hold the bead securely in that position, and use your dominant hand to wrap the wire around the frame again, as usual.

6 If you previously wrapped beads inside the frame, go ahead and make wraps on top of those wraps.

7 Bring the wire all the way around so that it is pointing outward again. (If you'd like, you can make more wraps here before adding another bead.)

8 String on the second bead.

9 Repeat Steps 5–7 with this bead.

10 Continue adding beads and making wraps until you are ready to end the wire.

11 Make three or more wraps around the frame wire, without beads.

12 Trim the wire tails at both ends of the frame and use chain nose pliers to squeeze down the ends of the wire against the frame, as usual.

You can use your wirework skills to create beautiful, stylish rings that don't require solder or molten metal. Once you master the basic technique, try experimenting with different wraps and embellishments.

SIMPLE WRAPPED RING

1. Beginning with a length of dead-soft 16-gauge wire that is about 10 inches long, center the wire across a ring mandrel with size markings, aligned with the mark for one-half size larger than you would like the finished ring to be.

2. Holding the wire against the mandrel with the thumb of one hand, use your other hand to bend back both ends of wire behind the mandrel.

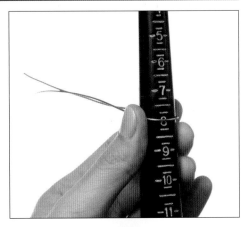

3. Pass both wires around the back of the mandrel, but do not allow them to cross over one another. (They should remain parallel.)

CONTINUED ON NEXT PAGE

④ While continuing to hold the wire
in place on the mandrel, bend
the wire ends back around to the
front of the mandrel and cross
them past one another there.

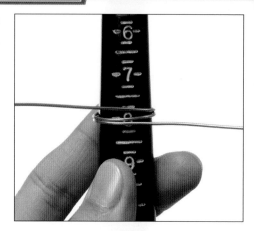

⑤ Bend the upper wire down over
the two lower wires.

⑥ Bend the bottom wire up over
the upper two wires.

7 Remove the wire from the mandrel.

8 Using your fingers or pliers, wrap each wire end around the ring two or three times, wrapping outward from the center of the ring.

9 Trim off the excess wire and squeeze down the ends with chain nose pliers.

TIP

Ensuring Proper Ring Size

A ring mandrel with size markings is useful for making rings of particular sizes, but it's not a foolproof tool. Notice that you make the simple wrapped ring by wrapping it *one-half size larger* than its finished size. This is to accommodate the added thickness of the heavy-gauge wire that you wrapped around the band in later steps. (It makes the inside circumference of the ring slightly smaller than it was at first.)

Keep this effect in mind when you design your own rings. Any wire wrapped around the ring's band will decrease its size to some degree. Even some large beads, if they sit low enough in the ring, may change its inside circumference. Keep your sized ring mandrel on hand when you experiment with new designs, and make note of any significant size changes that you experience during the process.

CONTINUED ON NEXT PAGE

WRAPPED BEAD RING

1. Beginning with a length of dead-soft 20-gauge wire that is about 15 inches long, string on one small- or medium-sized round bead.

2. Center the bead along the wire.

3. Bend up both ends of wire on either side of the bead.

4. Place the bead against a ring mandrel (aligned with the mark for the size that you would like the finished ring to be), with the wire ends positioned toward the back of the mandrel.

5. Bend the wire ends past one another around the back of the mandrel.

6. Bring both wires around to the front of the mandrel.

7. Position the wires so that each one passes slightly beneath the edge of the bead (between the bead and the mandrel).

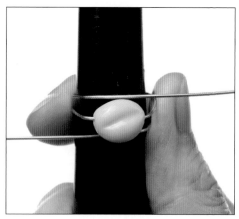

8 Bend the lower wire up against the side of the bead and over the wire that goes through the bead hole.

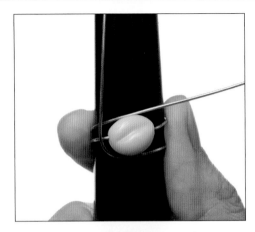

9 Wrap the wire completely around the bead one time.

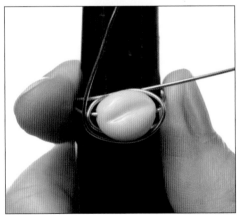

CONTINUED ON NEXT PAGE

10. Bend the upper wire down against the other side of the bead.

11. Wrap that wire completely around the bead one time.

    The two wires should now point in opposite directions (one up and one down) on either side of the bead.

12. Remove the ring from the mandrel.

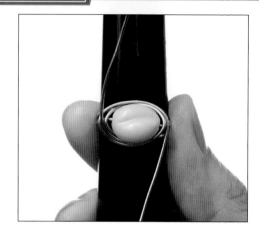

13. Using your fingers or chain nose pliers, wrap the wire on the left side of the ring down behind the ring band.

14. Wrap this wire securely around the band about three times.

15. Using the same technique, wrap the wire on the right side of the ring around the band on that side.

16 Trim off the extra wire from both sides, and squeeze down the wire ends using chain nose pliers.

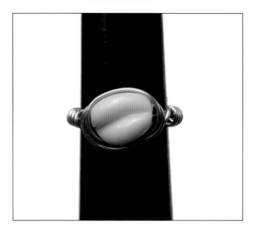

TIP

Instead of leaving your ring wires (called the ring *shank*) bare, try bundling them together and wrapping them completely with coils (see "Basic Coiling Technique" on p. 103). Just keep in mind that the coils will add some thickness to the ring, which will reduce its inside circumference and give it a tighter fit.

The *herringbone wrap* is a type of wire weaving. It creates overlapping wraps of wire that frame the bead in a beaded link. Use the *single-gauge* technique when you would like the wraps and end-loops to both have the same gauge of wire. Use the *two-gauge* technique for beads with larger holes, or when you would like to use smaller-gauge wire for the wraps than for the end-loops.

SINGLE-GAUGE HERRINGBONE LINK

1. Using 24-gauge wire directly from the spool, string on a round or rounded bead of your choice. (If you are wrapping very small beads, you can use 26-gauge wire instead.)

2. Use round nose pliers to make a loop at least 2 inches from the end of the wire.

3. Using the technique for making wrapped eye pins (see p. 57), make 8–10 full wraps at the base of the loop.

4. Trim the wire tail and use chain nose pliers to squeeze down the end of the wire.

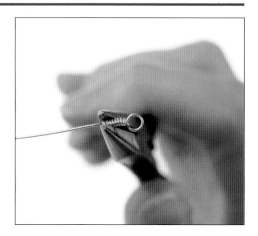

5. Slide the bead against the wraps that you just made.

6. Use the tips of round nose pliers (or a ruler or brass gauge) to measure the length of the wraps.

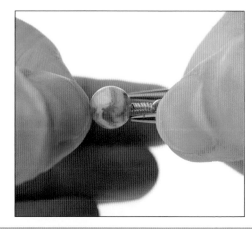

7 On the other end of the bead, bend the wire to a 90-degree angle at the same distance away from the bead as the length of the wraps on the first end.

8 Use round nose pliers to make a loop.

9 Make the same number of wraps that you made in Step 4, working back toward the bead. (Do not trim the wire.) If the wrapped portion of the wire starts to bend, stop and grasp it with chain nose pliers, as shown, and continue wrapping.

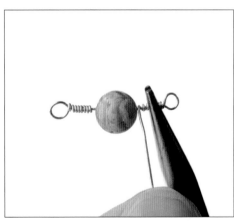

CONTINUED ON NEXT PAGE

⑩ If the wire from your spool has become bent or twisted, stop now and straighten it.

⑪ Use your fingers to wrap the wire all the way across the side of the bead.

⑫ Hold the wire firmly against the side of the bead with the fingers of your non-dominant hand, and use your dominant hand to wrap the rest of the wire over and all the way around the first wrapped coil on that end of the bead.

⑬ Now wrap the wire around the other side of the bead, in mirror-image to Step 11.

⑭ Holding the wire firmly against the bead, wrap the rest of the wire over and completely around the first coil on this end of the bead.

⑮ Wrap the wire back over the side of the bead that you wrapped in Step 12, positioning the wire directly behind and against that first wrap.

⑯ While holding the wire against the bead, wrap the rest of the wire over and all the way around the next coil on that end of the bead.

⑰ Continue working back and forth, from one end of the bead to the other, wrapping the wire against the side of the bead behind the previous wrap, until you run out of space to make further wraps at one end of the bead.

18 Bring the wire back to the other end of the bead, wrap it at least two times around the coils at the base of that loop, trim it, and use chain nose pliers to squeeze down the end.

The front and back views of a completed herringbone link are shown here. To keep connected links facing up, link them together using jump rings.

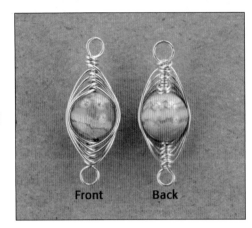

Front   Back

TWO-GAUGE HERRINGBONE LINK

1 Using 24-gauge or larger wire directly from the spool or coil, string on the first bead. (Use a gauge at least one size larger than you plan to use for the herringbone wraps.)

2 Use round nose pliers to make a loop at least 2 inches from the end of the wire. (For wire *larger* than 24-gauge, make the loop at least 2½ inches from the end.)

3 Perform Steps 3–9 of "Single-Gauge Herringbone Link" on p. 132.

4 Trim the wire close to the bead, and use chain nose pliers to squeeze down the end of the wire.

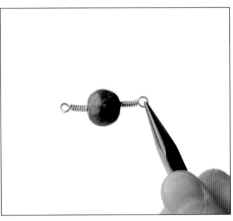

CONTINUED ON NEXT PAGE

⑤ Using smaller-gauge wire than you used for Step 1, directly from the spool or coil, bend-over about 1 inch of wire at the end.

⑥ Insert the coils on one end of the bead into the bend in the smaller-gauge wire.

⑦ Position the smaller-gauge wire so that the bend is 2 or 3 wraps away from the bead.

⑧ While holding the 1-inch wire tail against the loop at the end of the coils, wrap the smaller-gauge wire around the coils until you reach the bead.

⑨ Bring the wire around the side of the bead and wrap it over and around the first coil on the other side of the bead.

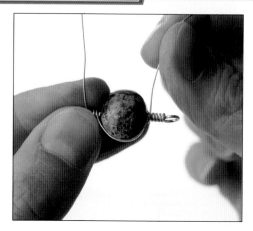

⑩ Go back to the other side of the bead, trim off the wire tail, and use chain nose pliers to squeeze down the end of the wire.

⑪ Wrap the wire around the other side of the bead, in mirror-image to Step 9.

⑫ Perform Steps 14–18 of "Single-Gauge Herringbone Link" (see p. 132) to complete the link.

A completed two-gauge herringbone link with 20-gauge and 26-gauge wire is shown here.

HERRINGBONE WRAP PENDANT OR CHARM

You can make a pendant or charm with herringbone wraps by eliminating the loop on one end of a bead.

1. Following the technique for making a single- or two-gauge herringbone link, create the first loop and the first set of wraps, and string on a bead.

2. On the other end of the bead, use flat nose pliers to make a bend in the wire the same distance away from the bead as the length of the wraps on the other side.

3. Use the pliers to squeeze the bend you just made into a very short fold, as shown.

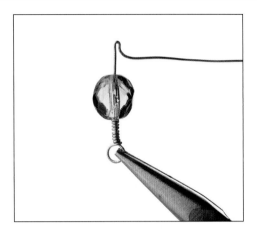

4. Grasp the end of the fold with chain nose pliers using your non-dominant hand.

5. With your dominant hand, wrap the wire toward the bead, making the same number of coils that you made on the first side of the bead.

6. Continue performing the herringbone weave as usual.

CONTINUED ON NEXT PAGE

7 When the folded-over wire is almost completely covered with herringbone wraps, bring the wire back over to the looped end of the bead and make at least two wraps just beneath the loop.

8 Trim and squeeze down the end of the wire, as usual.

More Advanced Wire Clasps

These clasps are slightly more complex than the basic hook clasps in Chapter 4. The *fold-over hook clasp* is a wrapped hook made with doubled (or "folded-over") wire. *Toggle clasps* are decorative alternatives to hooks. They are composed of two parts: *T-bars* and large clasp eyes.

FOLD-OVER HOOK CLASP

This example uses 20-gauge wire, but 22-gauge wire also works well.

1. Beginning with a 4¼-inch length of dead-soft or half-hard 20-gauge wire, use flat nose pliers to fold-over the wire 1¼ inches from one end. (Or, if you're using 22-gauge wire, 3¾-inch and 1 inch, respectively.)

2. Using round nose pliers, grasp the single wire just past the point where the doubled wire ends.

3. Use the pliers to bend the wire away from you at a 90-degree angle.

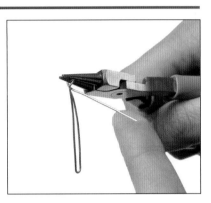

4. Without removing the round nose pliers, use the fingers of your other hand to pull the wire all the way around the pliers to create a loop.

5. Remove the round nose pliers and turn the piece around so that the loop is pointing in the opposite direction.

6. Grasp the loop with chain nose or flat nose pliers.

7. With your other hand, grasp the end of the wire tail with your fingers or with pliers.

8. Wrap the wire tail securely around both wires, below the loop, about four times.

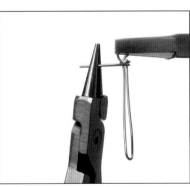

CONTINUED ON NEXT PAGE

9 Trim any excess wire tail and squeeze down the end against the doubled-wire base, as needed.

10 Grasp the center of the doubled-wire portion of the hook with the largest part of the jaws of the round nose pliers.

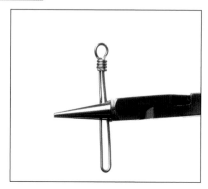

11 Use your fingers to bend the wire over the round nose pliers on both sides.

12 Grasp the very end of the doubled wire (the tip of the hook) with the round nose pliers.

13 Gently bend the tip of the hook outward.

14 Use your fingers to bend the wrapped-loop portion of the hook slightly toward the back of the hook.

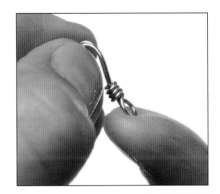

A completed fold-over hook clasp is shown here. It can be used with a simple or wrapped clasp eye, or with a large jump ring as a clasp eye.

SIMPLE TOGGLE CLASP

The T-bar of this toggle clasp is made of two separate pieces linked together. For a secure fit, the inside diameter of the clasp eye should be about half the width of the T-bar.

1 Beginning with a 1¾-inch length of 18-gauge wire that is flush-cut on both ends, grasp the very center of the wire with round nose pliers.

2 Use your fingers to bend both sides of the wire upward until they cross over the nose of the pliers.

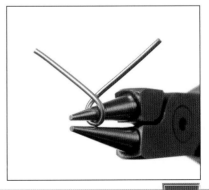

CONTINUED ON NEXT PAGE

3 Continue bending each wire downward to the side.

4 Check to make sure that the two side wires appear to be the same length.

Note: If one side is slightly longer than the other, trim it down now. If your loop is more than a little off-center, it's best to start over so that your T-bar will not be too short.

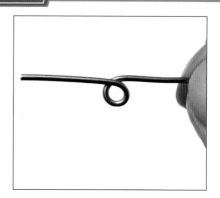

5 Grasp the end of one side of wire with the round nose pliers and create a small, upward-facing loop.

6 Turn the piece around and use the round nose pliers to create a small, downward-facing loop on the other side. Set this piece aside.

7 Using a 5-inch length of 20-gauge wire, grasp the wire with round nose pliers 1¼ inches from one end.

8 Bend the shorter end of wire over the nose of the pliers to create a loop.

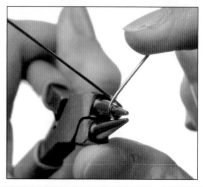

9. Turn the piece around so that the loop is facing the opposite direction.

10. Grasp the loop with flat nose pliers.

11. Use the round nose or chain nose pliers to wrap the shorter end of the wire around the base of the loop several times.

12. Trim off the excess wire tail and flatten down the end.

13. Holding the wrapped portion of the wire with round nose pliers, bend the long wire end to the side. After completing this step, the wire should look like this.

14. With the round nose pliers, grasp the single wire next to the bend that you just made.

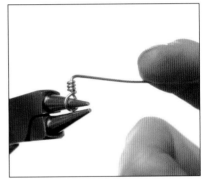

15. Bend the wire over the nose of the pliers to create a loop.

CONTINUED ON NEXT PAGE

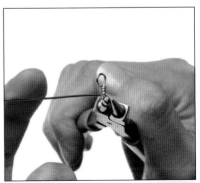

16 Pick up the T-bar that you completed in Step 6, and slide it into the open loop that you created in Step 15.

17 Turn the piece around so that the new loop and bar are facing the opposite direction.

18 Grasp the base of the loop with chain nose pliers, being careful not to crush or scratch the bar.

19 Use the fingers of your other hand, or pliers, to wrap the long end of the wire several times over the first wrap.

20 Trim the excess wire tail and flatten the end against the wraps.

21 Using the basic technique for making a wrapped clasp eye (p. 75 in Chapter 4), use 18- or 20-gauge wire to make a clasp eye with a loop whose diameter is about half the width of the T-bar.

22 Optionally, press the large clasp-eye loop against a mandrel to give it a slight curve.

WRAPPED TOGGLE CLASP

You can make the T-bar of this clasp using smaller, 20-gauge wire.

1 Beginning with 8 inches of dead-soft 20-gauge wire, grasp the center of the wire in round nose pliers.

2 Pull one end of the wire around the nose of the pliers to create a loop.

3 Remove the round nose pliers, and turn the wire around so that the loop is facing the opposite direction.

4 Grasp the loop with flat nose pliers, with the two wire ends pointing up and to the side, respectively (in an "L" shape).

5 Using the fingers of your other hand, bend the upper wire down over the lower wire.

6 Bend the other wire out to a 45-degree angle.

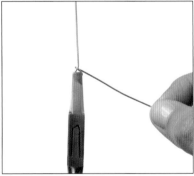

7 Go back to the first wire, and wrap it around the second wire two or three times.

CONTINUED ON NEXT PAGE

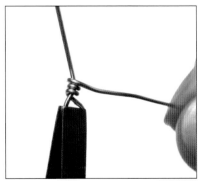

8 With the loop now pointing downward, hold the loop with the fingers of one hand, and use your other hand to bend both wires down to the sides.

9 Using flat nose pliers, fold over one of the side wires ⅜ inch from the loop.

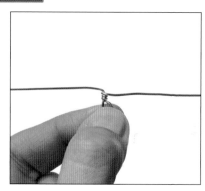

10 Turn the piece around and repeat Step 9 with the other side wire.

Note: Make sure that the side wires do not cross over one another.

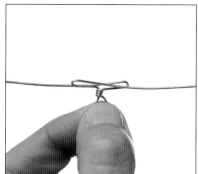

11 Hold one side of the piece firmly between your fingers.

12 Use the fingers of your other hand to bend down the other side wire in front of the bent wire as close to the loop as possible.

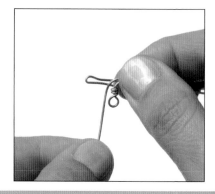

13 Using your fingers or pliers, wrap this wire around the doubled side wire until you are close to the end of the bar.

14 Turn the piece around and repeat Steps 11–13 on the other side.

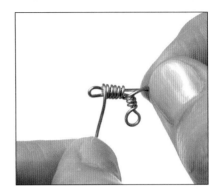

15 Trim off the excess wire at both ends, and flatten down the wire ends, as needed.

16 Perform Steps 21 and 22 of "Simple Toggle Clasp" to create the clasp eye.

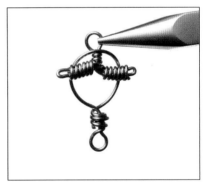

chapter 6

Wire Chains

With a little patience, you can use wire to make your own metal chains, link by link. Chains can be the focal pieces of jewelry, or they can serve as connectors between beaded links or bases for hanging charms. Here are some of the most popular wire-chain making techniques.

This basic chain is made entirely of jump rings. Try using 20-gauge rings for a finer chain, and 18-gauge for a bulkier chain.

1 Begin with two closed jump rings.

2 Use chain nose pliers to pass an open jump ring through both closed jump rings.

3 Close the open jump ring.

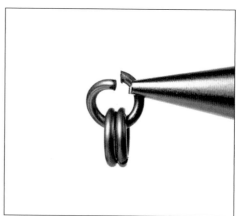

④ Pass another jump ring through the first two closed rings, and close it. You now have two links of chain.

⑤ Continue adding sets of two jump rings to the desired length.

A completed length of double jump ring chain is shown here.

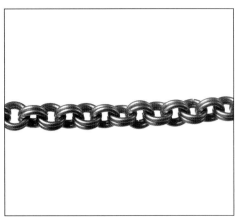

TIP

To give your chain a more finished look and make the jump rings less likely to open, hammer all of the rings before you begin assembling the chain. (See "Hammer Jump Rings" in Chapter 4.)

Make a Double Wrapped Loop Chain

To make this chain, you simply connect a series of two-loop connectors that look a lot like wrapped clasp eyes. Because the links won't pull apart, you can use small-gauge wire to make this chain if you'd like.

① Make several wrapped clasp eyes (see p. 75 in Chapter 4), but this time make all of the loops the same size.

② Link them together with double sets of jump rings.

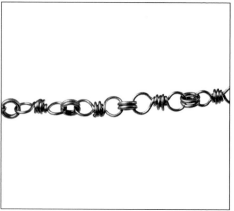

This chain is made up of closed "S" hooks that are linked together with jump rings. You'll need to use larger-gauge wire for the "S" hooks, like 18- or 16-gauge, to keep them from pulling open. Be sure to hammer the ends of the hooks for added strength.

1 Make some "S" hooks (see p. 82 in Chapter 4), and use your fingers or flat nose pliers to wiggle the loops closer together to fully close them.

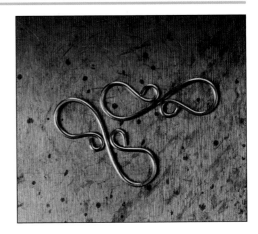

2 Link them together with double sets of jump rings.

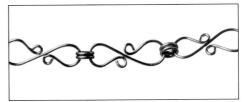

TIP

You can make this chain especially ornate by creating the "S" hooks with twisted wire or by wrapping them with coiled, smaller-gauge wire. (See the sections, "Twist Wire" and "Use Coiled Wraps," in Chapter 5.)

Construct a Double Spiral Chain

This showy chain has an ancient Egyptian motif. For efficiency, make the links first and then connect them all together.

MAKE THE SPIRAL LINKS

① Beginning with 4 inches of 19-gauge wire that is flush-cut at both ends, use round nose and flat nose pliers to begin an upward spiral at each end. (To review spirals, see "Spiral Head Pins" on p. 53 in Chapter 4.)

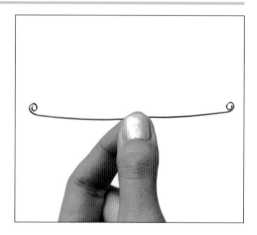

② Work back and forth between the two sides until there is a ½-inch space of wire between two equally sized spirals.

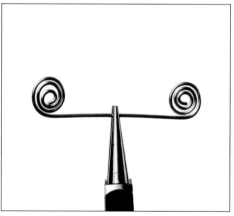

③ Grasp the center of the wire with round nose pliers, with both spirals facing upward.

④ Use your fingers to bend both of the spirals down below the nose of the pliers.

⑤ Repeat Steps 1–4 with separate pieces of wire until you have made the desired number of chain links.

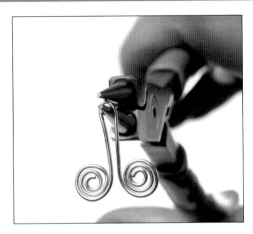

CONNECT THE SPIRAL LINKS

① Pick up one link and use flat nose pliers to fold over its loop, flush with the bottoms of the two spirals. The top of the loop should protrude a little above the two spirals.

CONTINUED ON NEXT PAGE

2 Pick up a second link and slip its loop through the end of the loop on the first link.

3 Use flat nose pliers to fold-over the loop on the second link, and lock the first loop inside. You should now have two links connected by their loops and facing the same direction. They should be connected loosely enough that the finished chain remains flexible.

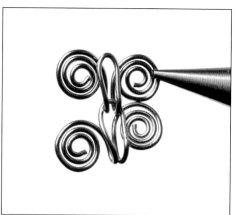

4 Continue attaching links in this manner until you have the desired length of chain.

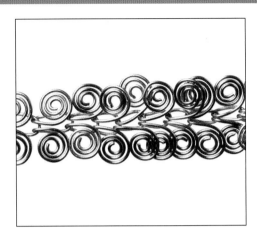

TIP

For a necklace or bracelet, the final link in the chain can also serve as the hook portion of the clasp. When you fold-over the loop on that link, leave it open; that is, do not press it completely down against the back of the link. Attach a large jump ring to the other end of the chain to serve as the clasp eye. To secure the clasp, slide the folded loop of the last link through the large jump ring.

The Byzantine is a popular structural chain that uses a large number of jump rings. You will use up the jump rings quickly, so consider purchasing pre-made rings in bulk or investing in equipment for making jump rings if you enjoy this technique.

1 Beginning with a supply of open 18-gauge, 5.5mm OD (outside diameter) jump rings, place two closed jump rings onto a safety pin.

2 After closing the safety pin, slip an open jump ring through both closed rings, and close it.

3 Repeat Step 2 to add a second closed jump ring to the original two rings.

4 Using the same procedure, add two more jump rings to the two rings that you added in Steps 2–3. You now have a three-link chain of double jump rings.

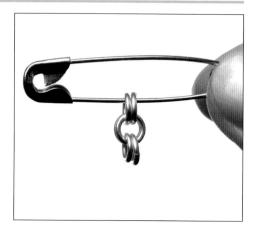

TIP

The Byzantine chain can be made with smaller-gauge jump rings for a sleeker look, or with larger-gauge jump rings for a bolder look. See the "Byzantine Jump Ring Size Chart" in the Appendix for recommended jump ring sizes to use with various gauges.

5 Grip the first two links of the chain (four rings total) with the fingers of one hand.

6 Fold back the last two rings in the chain, so that they fall to opposite sides.

7 Add the two folded-back rings to the rings that you're holding with your fingers.

8 Fold back the next two rings at the end of the chain as far as they will go. This will expose the next set of two rings below (shown in blue).

TIP

After completing Step 8, you may find it helpful to insert a long, narrow object (like an unfolded paper clip or a knotting awl used for beading) underneath the next two rings (in blue, above) to hold them in place while you add the next set of rings. Remove the object when the next set of rings is in place (Step 10).

CONTINUED ON NEXT PAGE

9 While still holding the chain with one hand, use chain nose or flat nose pliers in your other hand to thread a new open jump ring through those two lower rings that are now exposed.

10 Add a second closed jump ring to those two lower rings.

The chain should now look like this.

⑪ Attach two more links of two jump rings each to the rings that you added in Step 10.

The chain should now look like this.

⑫ Fold back the last two rings so that they fall to the sides, as you did in Step 6.

⑬ Fold back the next two rings as far as they will go, exposing the next two rings between them.

⑭ Repeat Steps 9–13 until you have the desired length of chain.

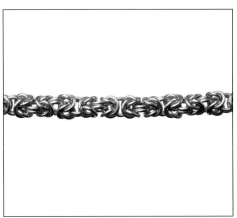

chapter

Using a Wire Jig

You can use a jig to create wire findings and components that are the same shape and size. Jigs are especially useful for making uniform connectors and ear wires, and most jigs have moveable pegs that you can rearrange to create your own unique designs. By creating jig patterns on paper, you can save your designs to use over again.

Wire jigs are easy to use once you get the hang of them. To begin, arrange some pegs on the jig by placing them into the holes. Next, anchor the end of your wire on the jig, and slowly wrap the wire around each peg in the direction called for by the design. Finally, remove the wire from the jig and trim off the extra wire ends.

ANCHOR THE WIRE

You need to anchor your wire on the jig so that the wire doesn't slip while you wrap it around the pegs. The simplest way to do this is to press the end of the wire firmly against the surface of the jig with the fingers of your non-dominant hand. Another way is to insert the end of the wire into an empty peg hole outside of the design before you begin wrapping.

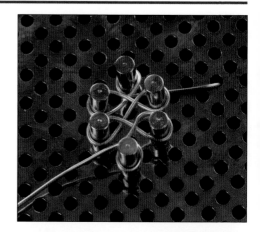

WRAP THE WIRE

Once your wire is anchored, you can begin wrapping it around the jig pegs. For best results, go slowly and keep the wire as taut as possible as you move it from one peg to the next. For small designs, or designs where the pegs are very close together, the wire may ride up to the tops of the pegs and threaten to pop off. If this happens, try pushing the wire down using the eraser-end of a pencil or the tips of flat nose pliers.

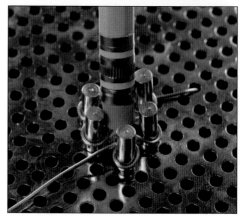

REMOVE THE DESIGN

Always lift your design off the jig slowly. Use your fingers to support as much of the wire as possible, so that it doesn't bend or stretch. You'll find that pegs sometimes stick in the wire loops and get pulled out of the jig when you do this. Simply tap them down again with your fingers, or take them out and replace them after you've removed the design.

Straightening a Jig Design

Large or intricate jig designs often appear bent after you remove them from the jig. With some designs, you can simply wiggle them into a flatter position using your fingers or flat nose pliers.

For a more dramatic effect, or when wiggling doesn't work, you can try hammering your design. Just be careful not to hammer too strenuously, or else your design will become distorted. For best results, use a nylon head hammer or cover the design with a piece of suede or leather before hammering, and focus your hammer strikes on the outer edges of the loops.

Make Connectors Using a Jig

You can use connectors as decorative elements or to connect other components directly or with jump rings. Just like beaded links, connectors can be made with simple, open loops or with wrapped loops. For sturdy connectors, use 20-gauge wire for small pieces and 18- or 16-gauge wire for larger pieces, and hammer the outside edges of all simple (unwrapped) loops.

SIMPLE TWO-LOOP CONNECTORS

A two-loop connector looks a lot like the Simple Clasp Eye made using round nose pliers in Chapter 4 (see p. 74). You can experiment to see which method and style you like best.

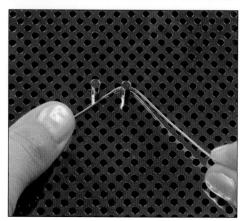

1. Arrange two pegs horizontally on the jig with one empty space between them.

2. Using wire directly from the spool or coil, place the wire diagonally between the two pegs, with the wire end reaching past the bottom peg by about 1 inch.

3. With the fingers of one hand, anchor the wire end against the jig.

4. Using your other hand, wrap the wire over and around one of the pegs.

5. Bring the wire back up between the pegs and around the next peg, in a figure-eight pattern.

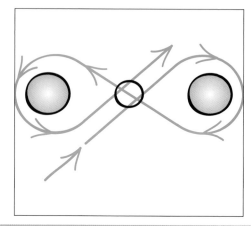

6 Position the wire diagonally between the pegs.

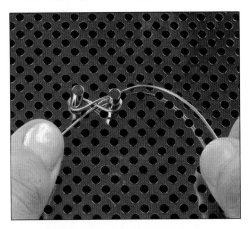

7 After removing the wire from the jig, use side cutters to trim off the ends of the wire at the base of each loop.

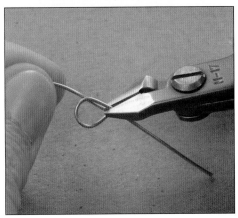

CONTINUED ON NEXT PAGE

⑧ Use flat nose pliers to wiggle each loop closed.

⑨ For added strength, hammer both ends of the connector on a bench block.

SIMPLE THREE-LOOP CLOVER CONNECTORS

You can use these connectors at the ends of double-strand bracelets and necklaces, or as necklace centerpieces to hold drops.

① Arrange three pegs on the jig in a triangle pattern, leaving one empty space between every two pegs.

② Using wire directly from the spool or coil, place the wire diagonally between the pegs, with two pegs on one side and one peg on the other.

③ Allow the wire end to reach past the bottom pegs by about 1 inch.

④ With the fingers of one hand, anchor the wire end against the jig.

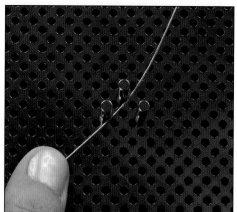

5 Use your other hand to wrap the wire over and around the top peg.

6 Bring the wire under, around, and over one of the bottom pegs.

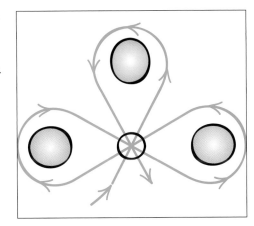

7 Wrap the wire underneath, up, and over the other bottom peg.

8 Complete the loop by bringing the wire down and out the bottom of the triangle.

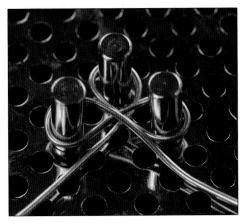

CONTINUED ON NEXT PAGE

⑨ After removing the wire from the jig, use side cutters to trim the wire at the base of the top and bottom loops.

⑩ Use flat nose pliers to wiggle each loop closed.

⑪ For added strength, hammer the ends of all three loops on a bench block.

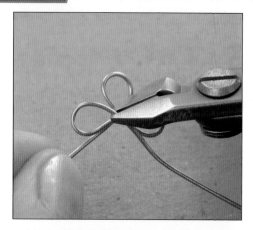

A completed simple three-loop clover connector is shown here.

TIP

You can make an eye pin that has a three-loop clover eye by trimming one of the wires in Step 9 an inch or more away from the loops. Then use flat nose pliers to bend that wire down about 45 degrees so that it serves as the straight part of the pin, centered between the first and last loops of the clover.

FOUR-LOOP CLOVER CONNECTORS

These connectors are similar to the three-loop version, but they're more versatile because of their extra loop.

1. Arrange four small pegs on the jig in a cross formation, with one empty space in the center.

2. Using wire directly from the spool or coil, place one end of wire diagonally between the pegs, with two pegs on either side.

3. Allow the wire end to reach past the bottom pegs by about 1 inch.

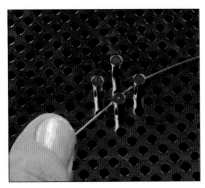

4. With the fingers of one hand, anchor the wire end against the jig.

5. Using your other hand, wrap the wire over the top peg.

6. Bring the wire down around the bottom peg in the opposite direction, creating a figure eight.

7. Cross the wire through the center of the pegs, and wrap it around one of the side pegs.

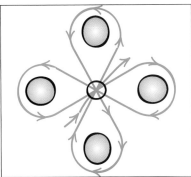

8. Pull the wire across and around the other side peg in the opposite direction, creating a sideways figure eight.

9. Position the wire diagonally through the pegs and out again at the top.

CONTINUED ON NEXT PAGE

⑩ After removing the wire from the jig, use side cutters to trim both wire ends at the bases of the loops.

⑪ Use flat nose pliers to wiggle the two open loops closed.

⑫ For added strength, hammer the ends of all four loops on a bench block.

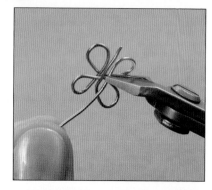

A completed four-loop clover connector is shown here.

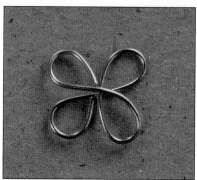

WRAPPED TWO-LOOP CONNECTORS

These connectors are more secure than simple connectors because their loops are wrapped closed.

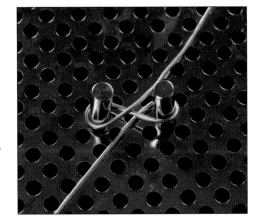

1. Arrange two pegs next to each other on the jig, with one empty space between them.

2. Using wire directly from the spool or coil, place the wire diagonally between the pegs, leaving a tail about 2 inches long at the bottom.

3. Using the fingers of one hand, anchor the wire end against the jig.

4. With your other hand, wrap the wire over and around one of the pegs.

5. Bring the wire back up between the pegs and around the next peg, in a figure-eight pattern.

6. After removing the wire from the jig, trim the wire so that it has about 2 inches of tail on its other end.

7. Using flat nose pliers, grasp one of the loops close to its base.

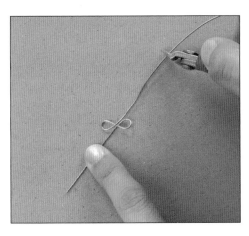

CONTINUED ON NEXT PAGE

8 Wrap the wire tail from that loop under and then around the base of the loop twice, using round nose pliers to grip the wire, if necessary.

9 After trimming off any excess wire tail, flatten the end of the wire against the coil using chain nose pliers.

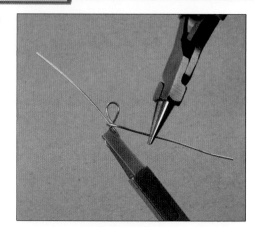

10 Turn the connector around and grasp the other loop with the flat nose pliers.

⑪ Wrap the second wire tail over and around the coil that you made with the first tail.

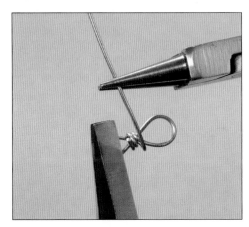

⑫ After trimming any excess wire, flatten the wire end against the coil as you did in Step 9.

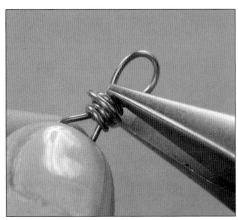

CONTINUED ON NEXT PAGE

13 File the wire end with a needle file to remove any sharp edges.

TIP

Making Your Own Jig

If you plan to make many pieces of the same component, you can save money by creating your own jig using a block of scrap wood and some nails. Use a pencil to mark the wood in the places where the pegs need to be. Then, select nails that have the desired widths of the pegs. Hammer the nails into the wood on the marks you made, leaving about a ½-inch length of nail between the wood and the nail heads. You now need to modify the nails so that wire can slip on and off of them. The easiest way to do this is to cut off the nail heads using a rotary tool like a Dremel, which you can purchase at most hardware stores.

You can use your handmade jig over again many times to make the same component. However, because the pegs are not removable, you'll need to make a separate jig for each type and size of component that you want to make.

WRAPPED THREE-LOOP CONNECTORS

1. Arrange three pegs horizontally on the jig, as shown.
2. Using wire directly from the spool or coil, place one end of wire diagonally between two of the pegs, leaving a tail about 2 inches long at the bottom.
3. Using one hand, anchor the wire tail against the jig.

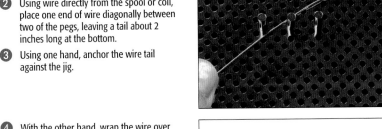

4. With the other hand, wrap the wire over the center peg, and then down again.
5. Bring the wire up, around, and over the next peg.
6. Position the wire diagonally and down between these two pegs.

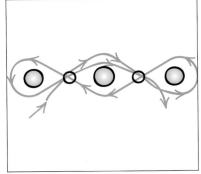

7. Wrap the wire around the bottom of the center peg, bringing it up diagonally on the other side.
8. Wrap the wire over and around the last peg.
9. Position the wire diagonally up between these two pegs.
10. Wrap the wire over the center peg, leaving it pointing downward on the other side.

CONTINUED ON NEXT PAGE

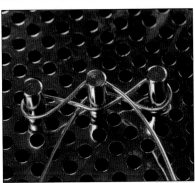

⑪ After removing the wire from the jig, trim the wire so that it has about 2 inches of tail on its other end.

⑫ Use flat nose pliers to grasp one of the end loops near its base.

⑬ Wrap the wire tail from this loop over and around the base of the loop two or three times.

⑭ After trimming any excess wire tail, flatten the wire end against the new coil using chain nose pliers.

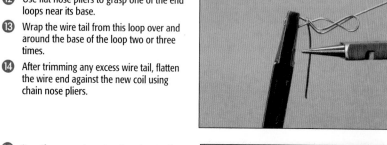

⑮ Turn the connector around, and grasp the other end-loop with the flat nose pliers.

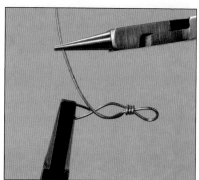

16 Repeat Steps 12–13 to complete this wrap.

TIP

Using Connectors as Spacer Bars

Wire connectors usually lie flat within a design to link components side-by-side. On large-diameter cord, like leather, they can also be used to hold multiple strands next to each other lengthwise.

To do this, simply string on a connector by threading cord through its loops. String on beads or tie knots on either side of the connector to hold it in place.

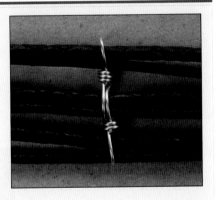

CONTINUED ON NEXT PAGE

CELTIC KNOT LOOPED CONNECTORS

These connectors make eye-catching focal pieces. Once you learn this basic approach, try creating them in other sizes and shapes using different diameters and arrangements of pegs.

1. Arrange six small pegs on the jig as shown.

2. Using wire directly from the spool or coil, place the wire horizontally beneath the top peg, leaving a tail about 1 inch long at the side.

3. Using one hand, anchor the wire against the jig.

4. With the other hand, bring the wire up and around the top peg and back down again.

5. Bring the wire up, over, and around one of the side pegs.

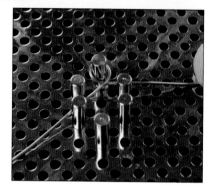

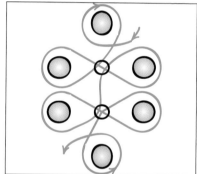

6. Cross over the center of the formation and wrap the wire around the opposite peg, creating a sideways figure eight.

7 Cross the wire over again and bring it down below the next peg on the other side.

8 Wrap another sideways figure eight around this peg and the peg opposite it.

9 Bring the wire down and wrap it all the way around the bottom peg.

10 After removing the wire from the jig, use side cutters to trim the wire at the bases of the top and bottom loops.

11 Use flat nose pliers to wiggle each loop closed.

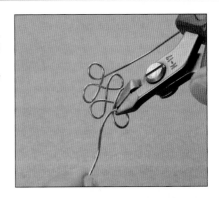

12 For added strength, hammer the outside edges of all six loops on a bench block.

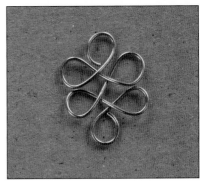

CONTINUED ON NEXT PAGE

SPIRAL-END LOOPED CONNECTORS

Follow these steps to add spiraled ends to a Celtic knot looped connector.

1. Arrange six pegs on the jig in the same formation as the Celtic knot looped connector.

2. Using wire directly from the spool or coil, place the wire end horizontally below the top peg, leaving a tail about 2 inches long at the side.

3. Using one hand, anchor the wire against the jig.

4. Perform Steps 6–8 under "Celtic Knot Looped Connectors."

5. After removing the connector from the jig, trim it off of the coil or spool, leaving 2 inches of wire tail on the connector.

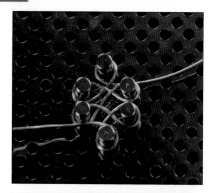

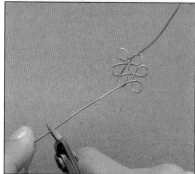

6. Using chain nose pliers, fold-over the tip of one wire-end in the direction shown.

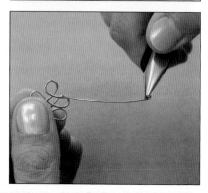

7. Begin spiraling the wire-end by performing Steps 4–7 for making spiral head pins in Chapter 4 (see p. 53).

8. Continue forming the spiral until it reaches the connector.

9. Create a matching spiral on the other end of the connector, rolling the second spiral in the opposite direction to the first.

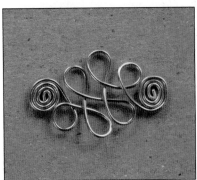

Form Ear Wires Using a Jig

Ear wires are easy to make and less expensive than their pre-made counterparts. Although you can make them using a mandrel (see p. 84–85 in Chapter 4), you may find it faster and easier to make them using a jig.

SIMPLE FRENCH HOOKS

1. Arrange one small, one large, and one medium peg on your jig, as shown.

2. Using half-hard 22- or 20-gauge wire directly from the spool or coil, use side cutters to make a flush cut at the end of the wire.

3. Grasp the wire end with round nose pliers, and roll them away from you to create a loop.

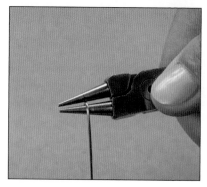

4 Place the loop over the small peg on the jig, with the loop facing downward, as shown.

5 Wrap the wire around and over the large peg, and down between the small and medium pegs.

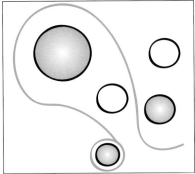

6 Pull the wire up slightly behind the medium peg.

CONTINUED ON NEXT PAGE

⑦ After removing the wire from the jig, use side cutters to trim the wire just past the final curve that you created in Step 6.

⑧ Repeat Steps 1–7 to create a matching ear wire.

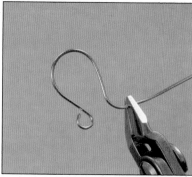

⑨ To trim the second ear wire, hold it up against the first one to make sure that you cut it in exactly the same place.

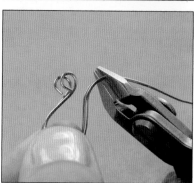

10 Place each hook on a bench block and lightly hammer the tops of the hooks in a direction moving away from you, until they are slightly flattened.

11 Optionally, turn the hooks around and lightly hammer the loops to stiffen them.

12 Use a needle file to smooth (or "debur") the edges of the tips of the ear wires.

A pair of simple French hooks are shown here.

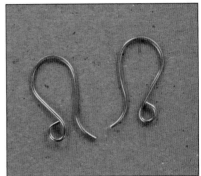

TIP

For the best results when deburring, hold the needle file at a 45-degree angle and gently file all the way around the wire tip. Then, lightly rub your finger over the end of the wire to see if it's smooth to the touch. If it's scratchy, continue filing gently at an angle until the wire tip is completely rounded and smooth.

CONTINUED ON NEXT PAGE

Form Ear Wires Using a Jig *(continued)*

CURLED-LOOP FRENCH HOOKS

This style of French hook is a little more ornate than the simple version.

1. Perform Steps 1–2 under "Simple French Hooks" (see p. 184).
2. Place the end of the wire on a bench block.
3. Slightly flatten the tip of the wire by lightly hammering in a motion that is moving away from you.
4. If needed, use a needle file to file the end of the wire smooth.

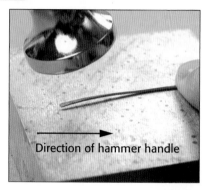

Direction of hammer handle

5. Grasp the wire end with the tips of round nose pliers, and roll them away from you to create a very small loop.
6. Turn the wire around so that the loop is facing you.

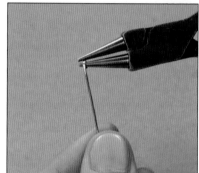

7. Grasp the wire with the round nose pliers just below the loop, and position the wire a little farther up on the nose of the pliers.
8. Roll the pliers away from you to create a second complete loop.

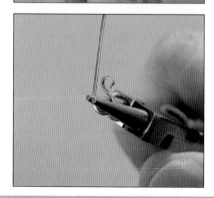

9 Before removing the pliers, gently pull the wire back and position it next to the first loop, as shown.

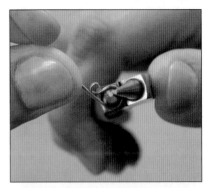

10 Place the second loop over the small peg on the jig with the loop pointing downward, as shown.

11 Complete the ear wire as you did in Steps 5–8 under "Simple French Hooks" (see p. 185–186).

12 Make a second ear wire to match.

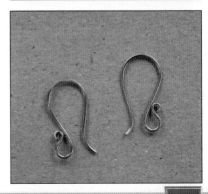

You can create your own unique components on a jig by experimenting with different peg sizes and configurations. When you discover a design that you really like, you may want to keep a record of it so that you can make it again. A good way to do this is to create a jig pattern.

DIAGRAMMING ON GRAPH PAPER

This is a very basic method for making a jig pattern. You simply draw-in the locations of pegs inside corresponding squares on graph paper.

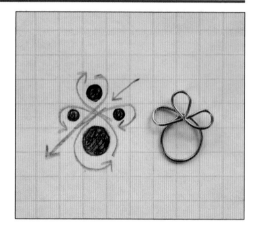

Begin by arranging the jig pegs and wrapping wire around them to create your design. Place a piece of graph paper next to the jig, and copy the locations of each peg onto matching squares on the graph paper. Allow each square to represent one space on the jig. Designate peg sizes by using varying sizes of circles or different letters, symbols, or colors on the paper. Use lines and arrows to show the path that the wire takes through the pegs.

To use the pattern, simply arrange pegs in the jig to match your diagram. Some jigs are even made of transparent acrylic, which allows you to place the pattern paper underneath the jig and follow the pattern as you work.

PEG-HOLE PATTERNS

Another way to create a jig pattern is to use pegs to punch holes in a piece of paper. For best results, only use this method with a jig large enough to hold two separate arrangements of pegs at one time, or use two jigs.

Begin by arranging the pegs close to one side of the jig, and wrapping wire to create your design. Place a sheet of paper over the other side of the jig (or on a second jig). Using new pegs, re-create your design in the paper by pushing the pegs through it and into the jig holes. When you're finished, you'll have a template that you can place over your jig to re-create the design.

To designate peg sizes on a peg-hole pattern, try color-coding the outsides of the holes using colored pens or pencils. You can show the path of the wire using lines and arrows, as you would with a graph-paper pattern.

CONTINUED ON NEXT PAGE

SOME WIRE-JIG PATTERNS TO TRY

Try making these connectors by following the graph-paper patterns provided. When you get accustomed to them, try altering them to create your own designs.

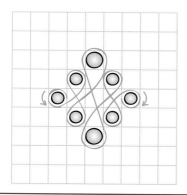

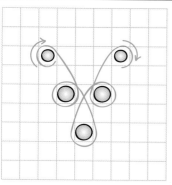

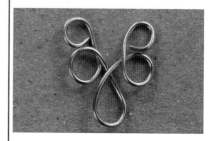

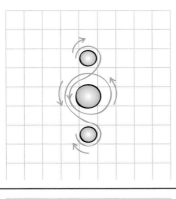

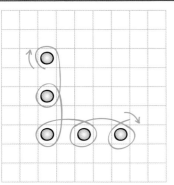

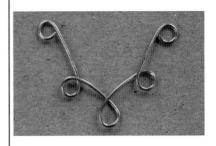

Appendix

References and Resources

American Wire Gauge Chart

Gauge refers to the size, or thickness, of wire. This chart lists the most common American Wire Gauges used in jewelry making, and suggested uses for each. The American Wire Gauge (or AWG) is the standard for wire sold in the United States; if you purchase wire in another country, be sure to ask your supplier whether they size their wire differently.

Wire Gauge	Actual Size	Diameter in Millimeters
12		2.05
14		1.63
16		1.29
18		1.02
19		.912
20		.812
21		.723
22		.644
24		.511
26		.405
28		.321

Diameter in Inches	Use for
.081	Solid cuff bracelets or bangles
.064	Wrapped bangles, heavy finger rings, heavy hook clasps
.051	Hook clasps, larger jump rings, heavy bead links for beads with large holes
.040	Jump rings, head and eye pins, simple bead links, heavier ear wires
.036	Same uses as 18 gauge
.032	Smaller jump rings, head and eye pins, smaller simple bead links, heavier wrapped bead links, lightweight hook clasps, ear wires
.028	Head and eye pins, heavier wrapped bead links, ear wires
.025	Head and eye pins, wrapped bead links, ear wires
.020	Standard wrapped bead links
.016	Small or fine wrapped bead links
.013	Wire crochet and weaving (advanced)

Often when you coil smaller-gauge wire on top of larger-gauge wire (see "Use Coiled Wraps" in Chapter 5), you must pre-cut a length of smaller-gauge wire rather than using it directly from the spool or coil. The charts on the next page provide a starting point for estimating the lengths of smaller-gauge wire (or "coiling wire") you will need for every inch of larger-gauge wire (or "base wire") that you want to cover. To properly use the charts, follow these steps:

1 Measure, in inches, the length of base wire that you plan to wrap with coils. If the base wire is part of a component and therefore difficult to measure, you can estimate its length or try pressing a measuring tape against the curves of the wire.

2 Write down that measurement.

3 Find the chart that best matches the gauge of your base wire. If that gauge is not shown, select the closest gauge.

4 Multiply the corresponding number in the right column by the base wire measurement you wrote down in Step 2. The result is an estimate of the inches of coiling wire you will need.

Here are some examples:

To wrap a 1¾-inch length of 18-gauge wire with 24-gauge coils:
1.75 (inches of base wire) x 11 (estimated inches of coiling wire needed per inch of base wire) = about 19.25 (19¼) inches of 24-gauge wire needed.

To wrap a ½-inch length of 20-gauge wire with 28-gauge coils:
.5 (inches of base wire) x 15 (estimated inches of coiling wire needed per inch of base wire) = about 7.5 (7½) inches of 28-gauge wire needed.

20-Gauge Base Wire	
Coiling wire gauge	**Estimated inches of coiling wire needed per inch of base wire***
28	15
26	10¼
24	9½

18-Gauge Base Wire	
Coiling wire gauge	**Estimated inches of coiling wire needed per inch of base wire***
28	16¾
26	12
24	11

16-Gauge Base Wire	
Coiling wire gauge	**Estimated inches of coiling wire needed per inch of base wire***
26	14
24	12½
22	10½

*Estimates include about 2 inches of wire (total) for the wire tails at the beginning and end of the coils.

Byzantine Jump Ring Size Chart

Use this chart to determine the approximate size of jump rings that you'll need to make a Byzantine chain using jump rings made from a certain gauge of wire. First, find the jump ring wire gauge you would like to use in the left column. The columns on the right provide recommended jump ring sizes, in millimeters, in both inside ring diameter (ID) and outside ring diameter (OD). When you purchase jump rings, check to see which of these two measurements your supplier uses.

	Recommended Jump Ring Size	
Jump Ring Wire Gauge	Approx. Inside Diameter (ID)	Approx. Outside Diameter (OD)
22	2.5mm	3.8mm
20	2.75mm–3.5mm	4.4mm–5mm
19	3mm	5mm
18	3.5mm–4mm	5.5mm–6mm
16	4.5mm	7mm

Millimeter and Inch Conversions

Small wire-jewelry making supplies and materials—like wire, jump rings, and components—may be measured in inches or millimeters, depending on the supplier or source. Here are the basic formulas for converting measurements from inches to millimeters, and vice versa, and a chart of the most common conversions for quick reference.

BASIC FORMULA

1mm = 0.039 inches (about $\frac{1}{32}$ inch)
Item size in millimeters x 0.039 = Item size in inches

1 inch = 25.4mm
Item size in inches x 25.4 = Item size in millimeters

Conversion Table			
Millimeters	**Approximate Inches**	**Millimeters**	**Approximate Inches**
1	$\frac{1}{32}$	11	$\frac{7}{16}$
2	$\frac{1}{16}$	12	$\frac{15}{32}$
3	$\frac{1}{8}$	13	$\frac{1}{2}$
4	$\frac{5}{32}$	14	$\frac{9}{16}$
5	$\frac{3}{16}$	15	$\frac{19}{32}$
6	$\frac{1}{4}$	16	$\frac{5}{8}$
7	$\frac{9}{32}$	17	$\frac{11}{16}$
8	$\frac{5}{16}$	18	$\frac{23}{32}$
9	$\frac{11}{32}$	19	$\frac{3}{4}$
10	$\frac{3}{8}$	20	$\frac{25}{32}$

Oxidization Methods

As it applies to wire-jewelry making, *oxidization* is the process of darkening, or "antiquing," metal by treating it with a chemical that causes it to react with oxygen. Most oxidizing chemicals are stocked by jewelry supply companies, and some even occur in non-toxic form in common household materials.

STERLING SILVER AND COPPER WIRE

The most popular, and fastest, method for darkening sterling silver or copper is to use a chemical called *liver of sulfur* (also called *potassium sulfide*). Most liver of sulfur is sold in "rock," or solid-chunk, form, but you can also find it pre-diluted in a liquid. The liquid form can be used straight from the bottle, but the rock form must be dissolved in warm water prior to use. (A typical recipe is to dissolve a pea-sized chunk of liver of sulfur in one cup of water.)

To darken sterling silver or copper jewelry, you alternate between dipping the jewelry into the liver of sulfur solution and rinsing it clean with water until you have achieved the desired color. You can then remove or lighten some areas by gently rubbing the jewelry with 00 (super fine) steel wool or a steel bristle brush.

Some downsides of liver of sulfur are that it is potentially toxic, it smells very bad, and it loses its effectiveness quickly after being dissolved in water or exposed to light. If you choose to use it, be sure to carefully follow the supplier's instructions. They will likely include wearing protective gloves when handling liver of sulfur, using it only in an area with very good ventilation, and storing it in a dark, dry place.

As an alternative to liver of sulfur, you can try oxidizing sterling silver or copper with a hard-boiled egg. Place the clean jewelry into a plastic bag containing pieces of warm, hard-boiled egg yolk. The jewelry should begin to darken within about 30 minutes, but you can leave it in the refrigerator overnight, or longer, for more intense results.

Note: *Keep in mind that the most important step in any oxidation process is cleaning the wire or jewelry thoroughly before you start. For most jewelry, you can use a mild hand- or dish-soap and water for cleaning, or a mild solution of vinegar and water.*

TIP

Because pure silver is very resistant to oxidation, these methods typically will not work to darken fine silver (which contains 99.9 percent pure silver). Similarly, sterling silver or copper that has been formulated or treated to resist tarnish (like the Argentium brand of silver) is difficult to darken. Be sure to use bare, untreated wire for any jewelry that you would like to oxidize.

BRASS WIRE

You can darken brass wire with the chemical *ferric nitrate* diluted in water. The typical recipe is about one tablespoon of ferric nitrate in one quart of water. To oxidize a piece of jewelry, you dip it into the solution, then take it out again and allow it to fully dry. Repeat this process as many times as necessary to achieve your desired color. Alternatively, ferric nitrate solution can be mixed in a plastic spray bottle and sprayed onto jewelry.

Like liver of sulfur, ferric nitrate can be toxic. Always follow your supplier's instructions carefully, including wearing protective gloves, using eye protection and possibly a dust mask (especially if you use a spray bottle), and ensuring adequate ventilation.

As an alternative to ferric nitrate, you can try darkening brass using vinegar. There are many different methods for doing this, and most artisans experiment to develop their favorites. Possibilities include simply brushing the jewelry with vinegar and allowing it to dry, slightly heating the jewelry in an oven and then applying vinegar, and suspending the jewelry above a container of vinegar on a piece of cheesecloth.

NICKEL SILVER WIRE

Nickel silver wire is relatively resistant to oxidation, but it can be darkened using a pre-made mixture of *nitric* and *selenious acids* available through larger jewelry supply companies. As with other chemicals, be sure to follow your supplier's safety instructions and use them carefully.

OTHER METALS

Other metals, in addition to those listed above, can be blackened using a commercial preparation called Antique Black. As its name implies, it generally creates a very dark finish.

Additionally, some wire is available pre-darkened. For example, you may be able to find copper craft wire that has been enameled in a dark color. *Dark steel*, which is sold at some hardware stores, is also pre-darkened; however, the color does not protect it from rust, so this wire must be kept away from moisture.

TIP

Some jewelry making supply companies offer pre-mixed formulations of oxidizing chemicals to simplify the oxidization process. Look for mixtures that are formulated specifically for the type of metal you would like to darken. As always, follow the safety instructions on the packaging carefully.

Polishing Techniques

Polishing is the process of removing tarnish and increasing shine. Most jewelry made from uncoated and unplated wire can be polished using a *jewelry polishing cloth*. You can purchase these cloths through jewelry supply companies, from jewelry stores, and sometimes at drug stores. Typically, one side or portion of the polishing cloth is embedded with a special polishing compound. When you rub the cloth over your jewelry, it polishes the jewelry's surface. The compound can leave a dull residue, which can be removed by cleaning the jewelry or by buffing it with a clean cloth or a piece of felt.

Another way to remove tarnish is to use a specially formulated tarnish-removing chemical for the wire material that you'd like to polish. For example, cream and foam cleaners are available for sterling silver, copper, and brass. You can also remove tarnish from copper (and sometimes silver) by dipping the jewelry into lemon juice or white vinegar, or rubbing it with a lemon wedge or ketchup.

If you need to polish bulk quantities of silver or copper jewelry or components, consider purchasing a rotary rock tumbler and a tumbling medium called *stainless steel shot*. Stainless steel shot consists of hard, polished pieces of stainless steel in a variety of shapes. When you place your jewelry inside the tumbler with the shot, some water, and a drop of mild soap, the tumbling action causes the molecules on the surface of the jewelry to align so that it becomes polished. Tumbling also increases the temper of wire. Tumble polishing is only recommended for solid sterling silver or copper, and it should not be used on jewelry that contains beads or stones made of softer gemstones or pearls, nor on beads or stones that are coated or "stabalized" with fillers. If you are unsure whether your beads or stones are coated or stabilized, avoid tumbling them altogether to protect them from damage.

TIP

Polishing can damage or remove the plating or coating on plated and coated wire. To minimize the need for polishing, use tarnish-resistant plated and coated wire whenever possible. If polishing is necessary, only polish them very lightly with a polishing cloth.

JEWELRY SUPPLY COMPANIES

Most of the tools, materials, and other supplies mentioned in this book are available for purchase through jewelry supply companies. Here are some recommended companies that offer mail-order service.

Rio Grande
7500 Bluewater Road NW
Albuquerque, New Mexico 87121
Phone: 1-800-545-6566
Web site: www.riogrande.com

Rio Grande is a large, wholesale supply company that produces at least three thick catalogs each year, including one devoted to "Gems & Findings" and one to "Tools & Equipment." You can order the catalogs on the Web site or by calling customer service. Although you do not need to be a professional jewelry artisan to order, there is a minimum order-size requirement. Call the customer service department for information about their current policies.

Fire Mountain Gems and Beads
One Fire Mountain Way
Grants Pass, Oregon 97526
Phone: 1-800-423-2319
Web site: www.firemountaingems.com

Fire Mountain Gems and Beads stocks a wide selection of beads, tools, and other supplies that are available through both their Web site and regular print catalogs. They provide combined discounts where you can qualify for various levels of wholesale pricing depending on the size of your order. The Fire Mountain Web site also offers many free tutorials and project ideas.

Otto Frei
126 2nd Street
Oakland, California 94607
Phone: 1-800-772-3456
Web site: www.ottofrei.com

Otto Frei specializes in tools, equipment, and supplies for professional jewelers and advanced hobbyists. They are a good source for wire-work tools like hammers, bench blocks, and mandrels. They also stock precious-metal wire.

CONTINUED ON NEXT PAGE

JewelrySupply.com
Roseville, California 95678
Phone: 1-866-380-7464
Web site: www.jewelrysupply.com
JewelrySupply.com offers all kinds of jewelry making supplies through its Web site, including tools and wire.

Jatayu
2247 San Diego Ave., Suite 237
San Diego, California 92110
Phone: 1-888-350-6481
Web site: www.jatayu.com
Jatayu was founded by wire jewelry artist and instructor Connie Fox. The Web site features a gallery of Connie's jewelry, free basic instruction, and her hand-selected wire-work supplies and equipment.

WigJig Store
P.O. Box 5124
Gaithersburg, Maryland 20882
Phone: 1-800-579-9473
Web site: beadstore.wigjig.com
Although WigJig is primarily a supplier of popular acrylic jigs, its online store also offers a wide variety of beads, findings, tools, and wire for your jig designs.

Paramount Wire Company
CBC Metal Supply
2–8 Central Avenue
East Orange, New Jersey 07018
Phone: 973-672-0500
Web site: www.parawire.com
Paramount Wire Company carries a large selection of wire, including brass, aluminum, nickel silver, stainless steel, plated metals, and colored craft wire in gauges ranging from as small as 32 to as large as 12.

The Ring Lord
290C RR6
Saskatoon, Saskatchewan, Canada S7K3J9
Phone: 306-374-1335
Web site: www.theringlord.com
The Ring Lord specializes in jump rings for chain mail artisans, but it is also a good general source for jump rings, wire, and components made from less-common metals including aluminum, stainless steel, and even titanium.

HELPFUL WEB SITES

Here are some jewelry making Web sites worth visiting for their helpful wirework resources.

About.com Jewelry Making
jewelrymaking.about.com

Art Jewelry Magazine
www.artjewelrymag.com

Beaducation
www.beaducation.com

BellaOnline.com Jewelry Making
Jewelrymaking.bellaonline.com

Creative Jewelry Making
www.beadjewelry.net

Eni Oken's Jewelry
www.enioken.com

International Guild of Wire Jewelry Artists
www.wirejewelryartists.org

Jatayu
www.conniefox.com

Sharilyn Miller's Wire Art Jewelry
www.sharilynmiller.com

Spiderchain Jewelry
www.spiderchain.com

WigJig
www.wigjig.com

Index

Perfectly portable!

With handy, compact *VISUAL™ Quick Tips* books, you're in the know wherever you go.

978-0-470-04578-7

978-0-470-07782-5

978-0-470-09741-0

All *VISUAL™ Quick Tips* books pack a lot of info into a compact 5 x 7 1/8" guide you can toss into your tote bag or brief case for ready reference.

Look for these and other *VISUAL™ Quick Tips* books wherever books are sold.

Read Less-Learn More®

Visual®
An Imprint of ⊕WILEY